BOTTLE DESIGN: BEER, WINE, SPIRITS

BOTTLE DESIGN:

Beer, Wine, Spirits

EDITED BY • HERAUSGEGEBEN VON • EDITÉ PAR:

B. MARTIN PEDERSEN

PUBLISHER AND CREATIVE DIRECTOR: B. MARTIN PEDERSEN

BOOK PUBLISHER: CHRISTOPHER T. REGGIO

EDITORS: CLARE HAYDEN, HEINKE JENSSEN

ASSOCIATE EDITOR: PEGGY CHAPMAN

PRODUCTION DIRECTOR: JOHN JEHEBER

ART DIRECTORS/DESIGNERS: B. MARTIN PEDERSEN, JENNY FRANCIS

GRAPHIS INC.

(OPPOSITE) DESIGN: TUCKER DESIGN / CLIENT: NEGOCIANTS NEW ZEALAND

CONTENTS

A CONVERSATION WITH MICHEL ROUX
BY VÉRONIQUE VIENNE..9

BEER...14

THE ROLE OF DESIGN IN CREATING BRAND IDENTITY AND MAINTAINING BRAND EQUITY
BY JOHN MAROTA, TOM ANTISTA, AND THOMAS FAIRCLOUGH.................................17

WINE..92

BOTTLE DESIGN: FROM FUNCTION TO FASHION
BY JOHN GRANT AND BARRIE TUCKER...95

SPIRITS...166

MESSAGE ON THE BOTTLE
BY MARY LEWIS...169

TRANSLATIONS AND CAPTIONS...228

INDICES..254

INHALT

EIN GESPRÄCH MIT MICHEL ROUX
VON VÉRONIQUE VIENNE...228

BIER...14

DIE ROLLE DES DESIGNS BEI DER SCHAFFUNG UND ERHALTUNG EINER MARKENIDENTITÄT
VON JOHN MAROTA, TOM ANTISTA, UND THOMAS FAIRCLOUGH..............................18

WEIN..92

FLASCHENGESTALTUNG - VOM FUNKTIONALEN ZUM TRENDARTIKEL
VON JOHN GRANT UND BARRIE TUCKER...96

SPIRITUOSEN...166

EINE FLASCHENBOTSCHAFT
VON MARY LEWIS...170

ÜBERSETZUNGEN UND LEGENDEN...228

VERZEICHNISSE...254

SOMMAIRE

UNE INTERVIEW AVEC MICHEL ROUX
DE VÉRONIQUE VIENNE...230

BIÈRE..14

LE RÔLE DU DESIGN DANS LA CRÉATION ET LE DÉVELOPPEMENT D'UNE IDENTITÉ DE MARQUE
PAR JOHN MAROTA, TOM ANTISTA, ET THOMAS FAIRCLOUGH.................................19

VIN...92

LA BOUTEILLE, AU-DELÀ DE LA FORME
PAR JOHN GRANT ET BARRIE TUCKER...97

SPIRITUEUX...166

HISTOIRE DE BOUTEILLES
PAR MARY LEWIS...171

TRADUCTIONS ET LÉGENDES..228

INDEX..254

REMARKS	ANMERKUNGEN	ANNOTATIONS
WE EXTEND OUR HEARTFELT THANKS TO CONTRIBUTORS THROUGHOUT THE WORLD WHO HAVE MADE IT POSSIBLE TO PUBLISH A WIDE AND INTERNATIONAL SPECTRUM OF THE BEST WORK IN THIS FIELD.	UNSER DANK GILT DEN EINSENDERN AUS ALLER WELT, DIE ES UNS DURCH IHRE BEI-TRÄGE ERMÖGLICHT HABEN, EIN BREITES, INTERNATIONALES SPEKTRUM DER BESTEN ARBEITEN ZU VERÖFFENTLICHEN.	TOUTE NOTRE RECONNAISSANCE VA AUX DESIGNERS DU MONDE ENTIER DONT LES ENVOIS NOUS ONT PERMIS DE CONSTITUER UN VASTE PANORAMA INTERNATIONAL DES MEILLEURES CRÉATIONS.
ENTRY INSTRUCTIONS FOR ALL GRAPHIS BOOKS MAY BE REQUESTED FROM: GRAPHIS INC. 141 LEXINGTON AVENUE NEW YORK, NY 10016-8193	TEILNAHMEBEDINGUNGEN FÜR DIE GRAPHIS-BÜCHER SIND ERHÄLTLICH BEIM: GRAPHIS INC. 141 LEXINGTON AVENUE NEW YORK, NY 10016-8193	LES MODALITÉS D'INSCRIPTION PEUVENT ÊTRE OBTENUES AUPRÈS DE: GRAPHIS INC. 141 LEXINGTON AVENUE NEW YORK, NY 10016-8193

(OPPOSITE) DESIGN: KROG / CLIENT: KRATOCHWILL

Commentary

KOMMENTAR

COMMENTAIRE

By Véronique Vienne

A CONVERSATION WITH MICHEL ROUX

Michel Roux, President and CEO of Carillon Importers, was the key strategist behind Absolut vodka's celebrated advertising campaign. For 15 years, more than 500 Absolut ads consistently featured a two-word headline under a photograph of a clear bottle of Swedish vodka. You had to be an illusionist of sorts to turn a plain, short-necked, round-shouldered, medicinal-looking vial into the sophisticated and distinctive icon that defined an entire generation of vodka drinkers. Michel Roux has that talent. By all accounts, he is a marketing wizard. "Presenting [ideas] to Michel is like presenting to God," said a young media buyer who worked on one of his other advertising campaigns. ■ In 1970, when he joined Carillon, Roux was its first salesman. Today he is credited for turning the Teaneck, New Jersey company into a top importer of spirits—the distributor of some of the most prestigious European brand names in the business, including Stolichnaya, Grand Marnier and Bombay. Ironically, Carillon no longer handles Absolut, the brand it made famous. In 1993, in a shake-up that surprised Madison Avenue insiders, the Swedish company that owns Absolut gave the account to Seagram; coincidentally, Carillon was awarded Stolichnaya, the premium Russian vodka. This sudden shift created quite a challenge for Roux. Everyone wondered if he would be able to embrace the brand that used to be Absolut's archrival. Pas de problème. Once a juggler, always a juggler. Without ever dropping the highball, Michel Roux conjured up his wits and went to work on the Stoli account. Today, the Russian vodka is poised to reclaim the market share it had lost to its Swedish competitor.

(PREVIOUS SPREAD) DESIGN: MICHAEL PETERS LIMITED. CLIENT: COURVOISIER S.A. ■ (OPPOSITE PAGE) MICHEL ROUX. PORTRAIT BY JOYCE TENNESON.
MICHEL ROUX IS PRESIDENT AND CEO OF CARILLON IMPORTERS. HE HAS BEEN INSTRUMENTAL IN THE DEVELOPMENT AND SUCCESS OF MANY EUROPEAN PRODUCTS IN THE US, INCLUDING STOLICHNAYA VODKA, GRAND MARNIER, ABSOLUT VODKA, AND BOMBAY GIN. ROUX HAS DISTINGUISHED HIMSELF AS A MARKETER, PHILANTHROPIST, SUPPORTER OF THE ARTS AND CIVIC LEADER AND HAS RECEIVED NUMEROUS AWARDS FOR HIS BUSINESS AND CIVIC ACTIVITIES.

VV: I understand that you were born in France, in the Charentes, not far from Cognac.

MR: Nothing is far from anything in that part of France.

VV: The French love to drink—particularly in that region. Do you try to share with American consumers your native appreciation of fine spirits?

MR: No, I don't. It's such a different thing. Where I come from, a glass of wine can last 10 to 20 minutes. The French sip on drinks. Americans, in contrast, consume alcohol very fast—they swallow what's in their glass to get a quick fix.

VV: Before joining Carillon, you managed nightclubs and restaurants in Texas. It must have been a culture shock at first.

MR: That's when I found out that the packaging of a bottle is just as important as the liquid inside. While the French care little about the look of the container, Americans are visually oriented drinkers.

VV: But there is that other content to consider—the mental, emotional and aspirational content of a bottle—in other words, its brand. I believe that's really your specialty.

MR: That's right. The brand is something that's perceived by all the senses. But first thing first—if the packaging is appealing, chances are people find what's inside more pleasing.

VV: What makes a packaging appealing?

MR: It must be intriguing—from the label to the shape of the bottle and the color of the beverage. For example, when we were reviewing the Bombay gin's blue Sapphire bottle, the research people told us that the tinted bottle made the gin look like mouthwash. Mouthwash? Absolutely not! Maybe a perfume—but certainly not a mouthwash. Actually, a lot of perfume bottles today are inspired by liquor bottles—and vice versa.

VV: You're right. Bottles like Calvin Klein's "cK One," Hilfiger's "Tommy" and Perry Ellis's "America" look like flasks of rum and bottles of vodka. And then, of course, there is Yves Saint Laurent's "Champagne." Maybe there is a reason for it. I read somewhere that in the past, *eau de Cologne* was made from grape spirit mixed with essential oils. It could be ingested as a liquor, or used as a fragrance.

MR: In my place in Provence, I make vodka flavored with the lavender that grows in my garden. It smells so good, you almost wish you could splash it on your skin. But I am happy to report that it tastes as good as it smells. By the way, did you know that Andy Warhol used Absolut vodka as a perfume? In fact, it was *his* perfume. I don't know if he liked the smell or if he was too cheap to buy a real fragrance. But don't mention this in your interview, because some readers will think that we are saying that it's OK to smell like gin and drink perfume!

VV: Do you have plans to market your own brand of lavender vodka?

MR: I don't think so. I have my hands full managing Carillon's brands. Marketing is like gardening: If you plant too many vegetables next to each other, they are crowded and none of them do well. Growing a brand takes years. It takes patience as well. Sometimes you don't even do that much. Sometimes it's best not to improve the bottle or the packaging. In fact, if you have a traditional product, you have to be very careful with changes. With Grand Marnier for example, we did clean up a part of the label a little bit, but we left the bottle alone—it represented such a standard of excellence to start with.

VV: So, what do you do? How do you take a product that's typically Swedish or French, for example, and make it part of the American culture?

MR: What is most difficult is to explain to the people who own a particular brand how it is perceived in another country. For example, it was almost impossible to explain to the Stolichnaya people why they had to add flavored vodka to their line of products. Emotionally, they resisted the idea. For them, it was a sacrilege. Just like it would be to my French client if I were to tell them that their *Château de Beaulieu* red wine has to be refrigerated and served cold.

VV: So, your job is to go around, explaining the American way of life to everyone?

MR: Certainly. That's exactly what I do. It's a thankless crusade. The success of a brand depends on how well I explain to people how their products are perceived in the United States. Sometimes I don't need to say much—but sometimes I have to make many trips back and forth.

VV: Do you travel a lot?

MR: I go to France and England six or seven times a year and to Russia almost every month.

VV: How do you do your research?

MR: My research ritual consists of being part of the action to find out what is really going on. My method isn't very sophisticated, but it works. I do it by myself. To build a brand, you must personally understand the psychology of the consumers. One of the things I do is talk to bartenders—and drink with them. In French liquor companies, salesmen have to be sent into detox at least once a year because their job requires they drink with bartenders and their buddies. Before they know it, they have fifteen drinks in their stomach. Here, in America, networking is a little less taxing: you can fake it by pouring the content of your glass in the rubber plant when no one is looking!

VV: Do you do traditional research, with focus groups and surveys?

MR: Yes. It's all bull as far as I can tell—but we do it anyway.

THE BOMBAY SAPPHIRE MARTINI. AS INTERPRETED BY ADAM TIHANY.
POUR SOMETHING PRICELESS.

THE BOMBAY SAPPHIRE MARTINI. AS ARRANGED BY ULLA DARNI.
POUR SOMETHING PRICELESS.

THE BOMBAY SAPPHIRE MARTINI. AS ENVISIONED BY MICHAEL GRAVES.
POUR SOMETHING PRICELESS.

THE BOMBAY SAPPHIRE MARTINI. AS SCULPTED BY ROBERT LEE MORRIS.
POUR SOMETHING PRICELESS.

THE BOMBAY SAPPHIRE MARTINI. AS EXPLORED BY RICHARD JOLLEY.
POUR SOMETHING PRICELESS.

THE BOMBAY SAPPHIRE MARTINI. AS ASSEMBLED BY GINNY RUFFNER.
POUR SOMETHING PRICELESS.

AUTHENTIC RUSSIAN VODKA FLAVORED WITH ALL-NATURAL OILS OF SRI LANKAN CINNAMON BARK AND CHINESE CASSIA.

AUTHENTIC RUSSIAN VODKA FLAVORED WITH ALL-NATURAL EXOTIC COFFEE BEANS FROM AROUND THE GLOBE.

AUTHENTIC RUSSIAN VODKA FLAVORED WITH ALL-NATURAL AROMATIC ESSENCE OF FRESH PEACHES.

AUTHENTIC RUSSIAN VODKA FLAVORED WITH ALL-NATURAL AROMATIC ESSENCE OF FRESH RASPBERRIES.

AUTHENTIC RUSSIAN VODKA FLAVORED WITH ALL-NATURAL AROMATIC JUICES OF FRESH STRAWBERRIES.

AUTHENTIC RUSSIAN VODKA FLAVORED WITH ALL-NATURAL EXTRACTS OF MADAGASCAN AND INDONESIAN VANILLA BEANS.

VV: What's the profile of the Stolichnaya drinker, for example?

MR: There are two distinct types: the first drinks Stoli and the second drinks *flavored* Stoli. The first is 35 years old and up, the second is younger—21 to 40 years old. Basic Stoli is cued to men whereas flavored Stoli is cued to women. Now, this is theoretical, of course. I believe that in life everything sorts itself out eventually—whether we monitor it or not. We have very little control over trends. In the past, for example, young people were looking up to older people to see what they were drinking—today it's the opposite. Older people are emulating younger people. Furthermore, at age 50 or 60, no one feels old anymore. So, it's tricky to try to target a specific customer. Who am I to stop a man from ordering a drink targeted to a woman? What I believe is that everyone is coming closer together—young and old, men and women.

VV: So, what makes a good marketer?

MR: Instinct. I never went to marketing school, but I know what ordinary people want, what makes them relax and what they are prepared to purchase to increase their sense of comfort. I see the potential in things. By the way, marketing alcohol doesn't necessarily have anything to do with drinking—thank God. For Absolut vodka, for example, we tied the brand to entertainment and fashion, because, in this particular instance, that's what made customers feel good about themselves.

VV: Looking back at the Absolut campaign, how do you feel about it?

MR: I can't take credit for creating the bottle, I only created its image. Not alone, though. There were a lot of people involved in the process—most of them these days are trying to take credit for the success of the campaign. That's fine with me.

VV: One of your biggest brands now is Stolichnaya—what are your plans for it?

MR: The Stolichnaya bottle isn't very intriguing. Take the label off and there is nothing much to it. It's almost like having a bottle of ordinary Russian vodka. But that's not necessarily bad. In the Cognac district, for example, fancy-looking bottles for premium cognacs are out while plain bottles are in. Simplicity is perceived as upscale. The Stoli bottle does not have very much to offer, but the label is different—and it makes what's inside look special. And of course, the "Freedom of Vodka" Stolichnaya advertising campaign, with its paintings by avant-garde Russian artists, adds to the sense of authenticity and uniqueness.

VV: If a brand is not advertised, can it grow?

MR: After reaching a certain plateau, it stops growing. The role of advertising is to sustain a sense of comfort in users. But a brand that's advertised must also be supported by word of mouth. Building a brand is a never-ending process of education—you do it bar by bar, one at a time.

VV: You talk to bartenders and they, in turn, talk to customers?

MR: Not only do you talk to bartenders, but you also hang around with their customers. You have to be mad enough about a brand to drink it night after night!

VV: Are you a publicity machine for your brands?

MR: You could say that. Although, recently, I am trying to cut down.

VV: Where do you find the energy to go out every night?

MR: It's a little bit like having sex at age seventy! But I am motivated by the fact that I love my brands and want everyone to love them the way I do. In our company, everybody becomes an ambassador for our products. It's that simple. Years ago, when I was working on the Absolut campaign, I remember going to some friends' house in the Hamptons. I walked into their place and the next thing I knew they were serving Stolichnaya. I turned around and left. I couldn't stand the fact that they drank my competition. Growing a brand *is* living it. I don't know why people sometimes don't get it.

VV: Growing a brand is like gardening, isn't it?

MR: For me, it is. I was born in the country and I am a man of the earth. Every morning I check to see how my salads, my strawberries and my potato plants are doing—I check my brands the way a peasant checks his fields. If you want something to grow, you must tend to it everyday. It's all about nurturing: a brand is not an inanimate object—it responds to your care. I like this line by French poet Alphonse de Lamartine: *Objets inanimés, avez-vous donc une âme / Qui s'attache à notre âme et la force d'aimer?* (Inanimate objects, do you have a soul/one that attaches itself to our soul and forces it to love?) Let me tell you, this business is not about drinking alcohol, it's about belief in something and living for it.

(OPPOSITE PAGE) CREATIVE DIRECTOR: ARNIE ARLOW. ART DIRECTOR: JANICE SALICRUP. PAINTER: LEONID GORE. BOTTLE AND LABEL DESIGN: LEONID GORE.

VÉRONIQUE VIENNE IS A WRITER WHO LIVES AND WORKS IN BROOKLYN, NEW YORK. BORN AND RAISED IN PARIS, FRANCE, SHE WAS TRAINED AT THE BEAUX-ARTS, ECOLE D'ARCHITECTURE, IN PARIS. FOR YEARS A PRACTICING EXHIBIT DESIGNER, SHE LATER BECAME A MAGAZINE ART DIRECTOR FOR PUBLICATIONS SUCH AS *INTERIORS, IMAGE, PARENTING,* AND *SELF.* VIENNE NOW WRITES ABOUT DESIGN AND CULTURAL TRENDS FOR NUMEROUS PUBLICATIONS.

Beer

BIER

BIÈRE

By John Marota, Tom Antista, Thomas Fairclough

One of the challenges of design is to make an impact—to emotionally touch and motivate an audience. At Anheuser-Busch and Antista Fairclough Design, designers make such an impact on millions of consumers every day. ■ Our world is constantly changing, faster than ever before. At work, computers and ISDN lines help us keep up with the pace. In the communication between packaging, marketing and design teams, files are sent on high-speed dedicated lines as quickly as they are produced. At home, 24-hour-per-day access to global news, satellite-dish TV, and pay-per-view mega-sports events reflects the speed and energy levels at which we live. Cultural events are also changing and shaping our visual environment, and with those changes, it's critical for consumer-goods companies to continually evaluate their brand and corporate identities. ■ A key to successful management of brand identities is to maintain their visual relevance. In other words, graphic design for effective brand identities in the mid-nineties must complement and relate to these cultural and visual evolutions. One prime example of how our visual environment has changed is sports. In the 1950s, baseball was "America's Game," a slower-paced sport for a slower-paced time. Today, it's no accident that basketball is billed as "America's Game." It is built around tempo, rhythm, and high energy—a slam-dunk of rapid-fire sensory stimulation. For product brand identities to be effective in this milieu, graphic design must pick up on these visual and attitudinal cues. ■ Within Anheuser-Busch, an effectively managed brand identity is Budweiser. Its famous red-and-white label

(PREVIOUS SPREAD) DESIGN: STEVE SANDSTROM/WIEDEN & KENNEDY. CLIENT: MCKENZIE RIVER CORPORATION/BLACK STAR BEER. ■ (OPPOSITE PAGE) DESIGN: ANTISTA FAIRCLOUGH DESIGN. CLIENT: ANHEUSER-BUSCH, INC. PHOTOGRAPHY: MICHAEL WEST PHOTOGRAPHY.

JOHN MAROTA IS THE DIRECTOR OF IMAGE DEVELOPMENT FOR ANHEUSER-BUSCH. HE OVERSEES THE CREATION OF ALL ANHEUSER-BUSCH PRIMARY AND SECONDARY PACKAGING, BOTH DOMESTIC AND INTERNATIONAL, ENCOMPASSING OVER 2000 DIFFERENT PACKAGE DESIGNS. ■ ANTISTA FAIRCLOUGH IS AN ATLANTA-BASED DESIGN FIRM. TOM ANTISTA AND THOMAS FAIRCLOUGH HAVE BOTH BEEN RECOGNIZED INTERNATIONALLY FOR DESIGN EXCELLENCE. SOME OF THEIR CLIENTS INCLUDE ANHEUSER-BUSCH, COCA-COLA, TEXACO WORLDWIDE, TURNER HOME ENTERTAINMENT AND LENSCRAFTERS USA.

design has become an American icon. Over the last 100 years, the label's basic structure and design have not been altered. However, Budweiser's brand identity has changed several times, constantly adapting to maintain visual relevance to the world's changing social and cultural environment. The Budweiser label has been made contemporary without affecting consumer perception of it. The type for example, a benign script face a generation ago, is now italicized, and Budweiser's can graphics now 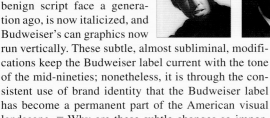 run vertically. These subtle, almost subliminal, modifications keep the Budweiser label current with the tone of the mid-nineties; nonetheless, it is through the consistent use of brand identity that the Budweiser label has become a permanent part of the American visual landscape. ■ Why are these subtle changes so important? Before any purchase, the steps a consumer goes through are awareness, interest, evaluation, trial, decision, and confirmation. All of our work in packaging development is targeted to the "trial" phase, that one moment in space and time when the consumer reaches out to pick up a product: "The Point of Purchase." This moment has become increasingly important, because consumers today are not only harder to reach, but are constantly bombarded with competing product messages; brand loyalty is no match for impulse. Therefore,

the package itself has to carry more weight for the responsibility of clearly communicating the product's position and swaying the consumer. ■ Effective package design communicates a product's attributes and benefits in a graphically relevant manner through the use of color, space, type, balance, and other visual elements. These devices are the vocabulary a designer employs to create a brand identity and an effective "package position." The process is like writing: one can't compose an essay without understanding grammar, and how one arranges the words determines the key communication. But grammar is not the end product of an essay, the idea is. Likewise with design, graphic tools are the building blocks used to communicate a larger message. That message is brand identity. ■ Our mission is to communicate brand equities through consistent management of brand identities and package position, all in a graphically interesting and relevant style. If a package does not create an emotional connection through its particular use of design elements, it won't be able to compete with the other thousands of consumer goods on the supermarket shelf today. Our objective is to get the consumer at the point of purchase to reach out for our product instead of the one next to it. When a design does that, it has truly made an impact.

DIE ROLLE DES DESIGNS BEI DER SCHAFFUNG UND ERHALTUNG EINER MARKENIDENTITÄT
von John Marota, Tom Antista und Thomas Fairclough.

Eine der grossen Herausforderungen des Designs ist es, Eindruck zu machen – ein Publikum emotional anzusprechen und zu motivieren. Die Designer von Anheuser-Busch und Antista Fairclough beeinflussen mit ihren Verpackungen täglich Millionen von Konsumenten. ■ Unsere Welt verändert sich unaufhörlich, und zwar in einem bisher nicht dagewesenen Tempo. Bei der Arbeit sorgen Computer und Internet dafür, dass wir am Ball bleiben. Zwischen Verpackungs-, Marketing- und Design-Teams werden Dateien in Sekundenschnelle hin- und hergeschickt, jede Entwicklungsstufe ist sofort für alle abrufbar. Zu Hause kann man 24 Stunden lang Nachrichten aus aller Welt empfangen, alle möglichen TV-Sender per Satellit und Mega-Sportveranstaltung durch Pay-TV – alles steht sofort zur Verfügung, und das ist bezeichnend für unser heutiges Leben. Kulturereignisse verändern sich ebenfalls und beeinflussen unser visuelles Umfeld; und angesichts dieser rapiden Veränderungen ist es für die Hersteller von Konsumgütern unerlässlich, ihre Marken- und Firmenidentität ständig zu überprüfen. ■ Ein Schlüssel zur erfolgreichen Betreuung von Markenidentitäten ist die Wahrung ihrer visuellen Relevanz. In anderen Worten, die graphische Gestaltung von Marken in den Mittneunzigern muss eine Beziehung zu den kulturellen und visuellen Entwicklungen haben, sie quasi ergänzen. In den 50er Jahren war Baseball «das Spiel Amerikas», ein eher langsamer Sport für eine langsamere Zeit. Es ist kein Zufall, dass heute Basketball als «das Spiel Amerikas» gilt. Dieses Spiel hat mit Tempo, Rhythmus und Energie zu tun – es ist ein anregendes Abenteuer für die Sinne. Um in diesem Umfeld erfolgreich zu sein, muss das Graphik-Design für eine Biermarke die visuellen und emotionalen Stichworte aufgreifen. ■ Ein Beispiel

für richtiges Marken-Management ist Budweiser-Bier von Anheuser-Busch. Ihr berühmtes rotweisses Etikett ist zu einer amerikanischen Ikone geworden. In den letzten 100 Jahren wurden die Grundstruktur und das Design nicht wirklich verändert. Das Markenimage von Budweiser wurde trotzdem mehrmals verändert, indem es konstant angepasst wurde, um im sich verändernden sozialen und kulturellen Umfeld optisch relevant zu bleiben. Das Etikett wurde der Zeit angepasst, ohne dass die Konsumenten es merkten. Die Typographie zum Beispiel – eine harmlose Schrift von vor 20 Jahren – ist jetzt kursiv und auf den Dosen für Budweiser-Bier vertikal ausgerichtet. Diese sanften, fast unterschwelligen Veränderungen haben Budweiser dem Ton der Mittneunziger angepasst, und trotzdem ist es die Kontinuität des Auftritts, die Budweiser zu einem nicht wegzudenkenden Teil der visuellen Landschaft Amerikas machte. ■ Warum sind diese sanften Veränderungen so wichtig? Bevor es zu irgendeinem Kauf kommt, müssen folgende Voraussetzungen beim Konsumenten erfüllt sein: Bewusstsein, Interesse, Auswertung, Prüfung, Entscheidung und Bestätigung. Unsere ganze Arbeit in der Entwicklung von Verpackungen konzentriert sich auf Ort und Zeit der «Prüfungsphase», jenem Moment, in dem der Konsument das Produkt in die Hand nimmt, im Laden, am «Point of Purchase». ■ Dieser Augenblick wird immer wichtiger, nicht nur weil man die Konsumenten heute schwerer erreicht, sondern auch weil sie konstant mit Botschaften der Konkurrenz bombardiert werden; Markenloyalität hat nichts mit impulsiven Entscheidungen zu tun. Darum muss die Verpackung vor allem darauf ausgerichtet sein, die Position des Produktes klar zu formulieren und den Konsumenten zu überzeugen. ■ Eine wirkungsvolle Verpackung

JOHN MAROTA IST DIRECTOR OF IMAGE DEVELOPMENT BEI DER BRAUEREI ANHEUSER-BUSCH. ER IST FÜR DIE GESTALTUNG VON INSGESAMT 2000 VERSCHIEDENEN VERPACKUNGEN FÜR DEN INLANDMARKT UND DEN EXPORT ZUSTÄNDIG. ■ ANTISTA FAIRCLOUGH IST EINE DESIGNFIRMA IN ATLANTA, USA. **TOM ANTISTA** UND **THOMAS FAIRCLOUGH** HABEN SICH INTERNATIONAL EINEN RUF ERWORBEN. ZU IHREN KUNDEN GEHÖREN ANHEUSER-BUSCH, COCA-COLA, TEXACO WORLDWIDE, TURNER HOME ENTERTAINMENT UND LENSCRAFTERS USA.

informiert über die Eigenschaften und Vorteile des Produktes auf graphisch relevante Art mit Hilfe von Farbe, Komposition, Typographie und anderer visueller Elemente. Dies ist das Vokabular, das ein Designer einsetzt, um eine Markenidentität und eine wirkungsvolle Verpackung zu schaffen. Es ist wie beim Schreiben: man kann keinen Aufsatz ohne Kenntnis der Grammatik schreiben, die Botschaft hängt davon ab, wie die Worte aneinander gereiht sind. Aber Grammatik ist nicht Gegenstand des Aufsatzes, sondern die Idee. Ebenso sind beim Graphik-Design die verschiedenen Elemente nur Instrumente, mit deren Hilfe die Botschaft kommuniziert wird. Diese Botschaft ist die Markenidentität. ■ Unsere Aufgabe besteht darin, den Wert einer Marke mitzuteilen, und zwar durch kontinuierliche Anpassung des Markenauftritts und der Verpackung auf graphisch interessante und relevante Art. Wenn eine Verpackung durch den besonderen Einsatz graphischer Elemente keine emotionale Verbindung zum Konsumenten herstellt, wird sie es nicht schaffen, sich gegen die anderen 17'000 Produkte in den Gestellen eines modernen Supermarktes durchzusetzen. Unser Ziel ist es, den Konsumenten im Laden anzusprechen, so dass er zu unserem Produkt und nicht zu dem daneben greift. Wenn das Design dies schafft, hat es wirklich Wirkung.

LE RÔLE DU DESIGN DANS LA CRÉATION ET LE DÉVELOPPEMENT D'UNE IDENTITÉ DE MARQUE
par John Marota, Tom Antista et Thomas Fairclough

L'un des plus grands défis du design est d'exercer un impact, c'est-à-dire de toucher émotionnellement le public cible et de le motiver. Les designers d'Anheuser-Busch et d'Antista Fairclough influencent ainsi tous les jours des millions de consommateurs avec leurs packagings. ■ Notre monde se trouve en constante évolution, et tout va de plus en plus vite. Au travail, les ordinateurs et les réseaux câblés nous permettent de suivre la cadence. Les équipes du packaging, du marketing et les designers peuvent se transmettre des fichiers ou accéder à des données en l'espace de quelques secondes. Chez soi, les satellites de communication permettent de capter des informations du monde entier 24 heures sur 24, de zapper au gré de ses envies ou d'assister de manière ciblée aux grandes manifestations sportives grâce à la nouvelle télé à la carte: tout est immédiatement disponible, une caractéristique de notre époque. Les événements culturels changent eux aussi et influencent notre environnement visuel. Compte tenu de ces changements rapides, il est primordial pour les fabricants de biens de consommation de vérifier régulièrement l'impact de leurs identités visuelle et institutionnelle. ■ La clé pour bien gérer une identité de marque consiste à préserver sa pertinence visuelle. En clair, cela signifie que le concept graphique d'une marque réalisé dans les années 90 doit être en phase avec l'évolution de la culture et de l'environnement visuel, voire les compléter. Dans les années 50, l'Amérique a connu un engouement sans précédent pour le base-ball. Ce sport, plutôt lent, correspondait à une époque où les choses évoluaient lentement. Aujourd'hui, le basket a supplanté le base-ball, et cela n'est pas un hasard. Musclé, rythmé et dynamique, ce sport est un véritable cocktail énergisant. Pour s'affirmer avec succès dans ce contexte, le graphisme d'une marque doit intégrer ces qualités visuelles et émotionnelles. ■ Distribuée par Anheuser-Busch, la bière Budweiser est un exemple probant d'une bonne gestion de marque. La célèbre étiquette rouge et blanc est devenue un symbole de l'Amérique. Au cours des 100 dernières années, le concept de base et le graphisme de la marque n'ont subi aucune modification notoire. L'identité visuelle de la célèbre bière a toutefois été toilettée à plusieurs reprises afin de garantir sa cohérence visuelle dans un environnement socioculturel en constante évolution. L'étiquette a ainsi été reliftée en fonction de l'air du temps sans que les consommateurs ne le remarquent. La typographie – un caractère datant de vingt ans – a été modifiée, et le nom de la bière s'affiche désormais en italique sur les canettes. Effectuées en douceur, ces modifications quasi subliminales ont su traduire l'esprit des années 90; néanmoins, c'est grâce à un concept développé de façon cohérente au fil des ans que la marque Budweiser fait désormais partie du paysage visuel de l'Amérique. ■ En quoi ces changements si subtils sont-ils si importants? Avant de se décider à l'achat, le consommateur passe par différents «états d'âme»: le produit attire son attention, son intérêt est éveillé. Il juge, prend sa décision et met l'article dans son panier. Tout notre travail dans le développement de packagings est axé sur la phase du «jugement», cet instant unique dans le temps et l'espace où le consommateur tend la main pour s'emparer du produit. ■ Cet instant revêt une importance accrue dans la mesure où, d'une part, les consommateurs d'aujourd'hui sont plus difficiles à séduire et, d'autre part, ils sont constamment bombardés par les messages de la concurrence; or, la fidélité à une marque n'est pas basée sur les actes d'achat impulsifs, spontanés. C'est pourquoi le packaging joue un rôle fondamental en permettant de positionner clairement un produit et de séduire le consommateur. ■ Un bon packaging informe des caractéristiques et des qualités d'un produit grâce à un graphisme adéquat réalisé à l'aide de couleurs, de la composition, de la typographie et d'autres éléments visuels. Ces éléments constituent le vocabulaire utilisé par un designer pour créer une identité de marque et un packaging efficace. Ce processus est analogue à celui de l'écriture: on ne peut rédiger une composition sans connaître les règles de la grammaire, et le sens du message dépend de l'ordre des mots. Mais la grammaire n'est pas une finalité en soi, ce sont les idées qui font la valeur d'un texte. Il en va de même du design, les éléments graphiques mis en œuvre sont les outils permettant de communiquer un message plus important. Ce message, c'est l'identité de marque. ■ Notre mission consiste à communiquer la valeur d'une marque en développant de manière cohérente identité visuelle et packaging grâce à un graphisme ad hoc. Si un packaging ne parvient pas à créer une relation émotionnelle avec les éléments graphiques utilisés, il a peu de chances de se démarquer parmi les quelque 17'000 produits proposés dans les linéaires d'un supermarché. Notre vocation est de convaincre le consommateur sur le point de vente de choisir notre produit plutôt que celui de la marque concurrente. Lorsqu'un design permet d'atteindre cet objectif, on peut dire qu'il a accompli sa mission.

(OPPOSITE, LEFT) TOM ANTISTA. PHOTO: MICHAEL WEST. (CENTER) JOHN MAROTA. PHOTO: PHILIP SOULBERG. (RIGHT) THOMAS FAIRCLOUGH. PHOTO: MICHAEL WEST.

JOHN MAROTA EST DIRECTEUR D'IMAGE DEVELOPMENT POUR ANHEUSER-BUSCH. IL SUPERVISE LA CRÉATION DE PLUS DE 2000 PACKAGINGS DESTINÉS AU MARCHÉ AMÉRICAIN ET À L'EXPORTATION. ■ ANTISTA FAIRCLOUGH EST UNE SOCIÉTÉ DE DESIGN ÉTABLIE À ATLANTA. TOM ANTISTA ET THOMAS FAIRCLOUGH SE SONT TAILLÉS UNE RÉPUTATION INTERNATIONALE POUR LA QUALITÉ DE LEURS RÉALISATIONS. LEUR CLIENTÈLE COMPREND DES NOMS PRESTIGIEUX, TELS QUE ANHEUSER-BUSCH, COCA-COLA, TEXACO WORLDWIDE, TURNER HOME ENTERTAINMENT ET LENSCRAFTERS USA.

Design
Cahan & Associates
Client
Boisset USA

Design
Cahan & Associates
Client
Boisset USA

Design
Cahan & Associates
Client
Boisset USA

Design
Cahan & Associates
Client
Boisset USA

(OPPOSITE PAGE)

Design
Design in Action

Client
Scottish Courage

Design
Landor Associates, Seattle

Client
Bert Grant's

Design
Partners Design, Inc.
Client
Neversink Brewery

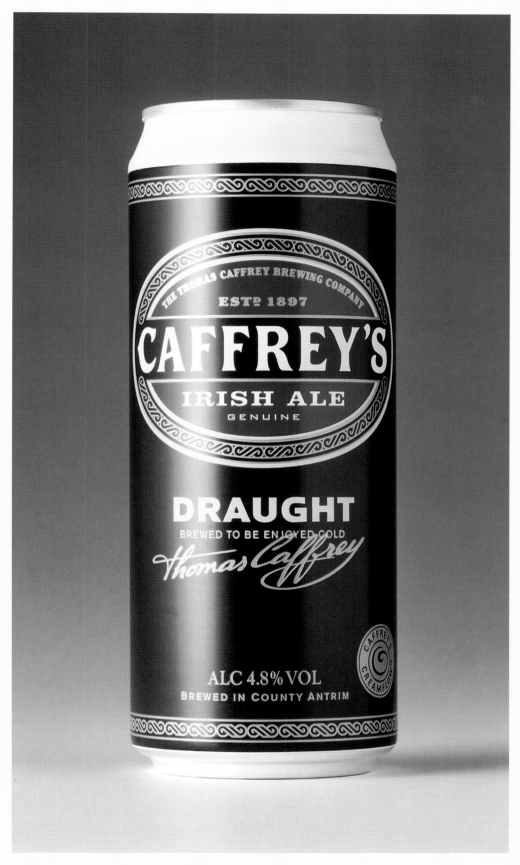

Design
Lewis Moberly
Client
Bass Plc.

Design
Duffy Design
Client
Flagstone Brewery

(THIS PAGE)
Design
Duffy Design
Client
The Stroh Brewery

Design
Duffy Design
Client
The Stroh Brewery

Design
Duffy Design
Client
Molson Brewery

Design
Duffy Design
Client
The Stroh Brewery

Design
Mires Design
Client
Bordeaux Printers

(OPPOSITE PAGE)
Design
Antista Fairclough Design
Client
Anheuser-Busch, Inc.

(THIS PAGE)
Design
Antista Fairclough Design
Client
Anheuser-Busch, Inc.

Design
Antista Fairclough Design
Client
Anheuser-Busch, Inc.

Design
Antista Fairclough Design
Client
Anheuser-Busch, Inc.

(TOP)
Design
Antista Fairclough Design
Client
Anheuser-Busch Inc.

(MIDDLE)
Design
Primo Angeli Inc.
Client
Hal Riney & Partners

(BOTTOM)
Design
Antista Fairclough Design
Client
Anheuser-Busch, Inc.

(OPPOSITE PAGE)
Design
Primo Angeli Inc.
Client
Hal Riney & Partners

NORTHERN PLAINS
BREWING COMPANY

RED RIVER
V · A · L · L · E · Y

S · E · L · E · C · T
RED LAGER

*Traditionally Brewed
with the Finest Hops, Pure
Water and Red River
Valley Malting Barley*

N° DAKOTA RESERVE

12 FL. OZ.

355ml BEER

Design
Cawrse & Effect
Client
Self-promotion

(TOP)	(MIDDLE)	(BOTTOM)
Design	*Design*	*Design*
Curtis Design	DiDonato Associates	Michael Osborne Design
Client	*Client*	*Client*
Miller Brewing Company	Goose Island Beer Company	St. Stan's Brewing Co.

Design
Lewis Moberly
Client
Bass Plc.

Design
Michael Peters Ltd.
Client
Sibra S.A.

(THIS SPREAD)
Design
Sibley/Peteet Design
Client
The Gambrinus Company

Design
EH6 Design Consultants
Client
Tennent Caledonian Breweries

Design
Division
Client
Saku Brewery, Ltd.

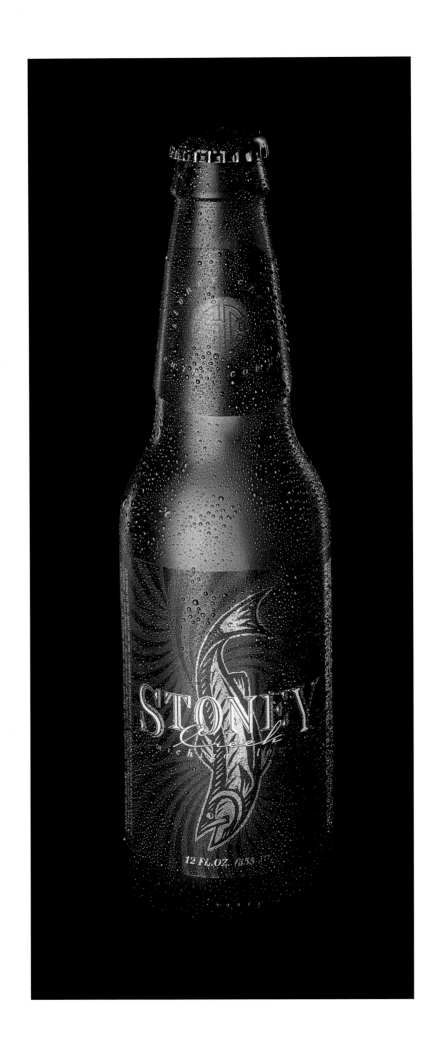

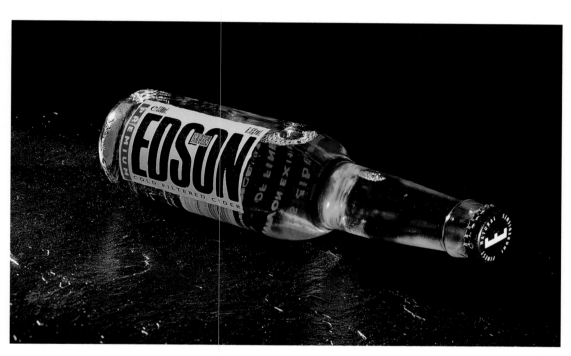

(OPPOSITE PAGE)

Design
Coomes Dudek

Client
Stoney Creek

Design
Tutssels

Client
Inch's Cider Ltd.

Design
Cato Design Inc.
Client
Foster's

Design
Wickens Tutt Southgate
Client
Allied Breweries

Design
Cato Design Inc.
Client
Foster's

Design
Sterling Group
Client
Miller Brewing Co.

Design
Cato Design Inc.
Client
Cascade Brewery

Design
Primo Angeli Inc.
Client
Matilda Bay Brewing Company

Design
Cato Design Inc.
Client
DB Breweries Limited

Design
Cato Design Inc.
Client
South Pacific Brewery

(OPPOSITE PAGE)

Design
Ziggurat

Client
Asda Stores Plc

Design
Group M

Client
Dock Street
Brewing Company

Design
Pentagram Design
Client
Flying Fish Brewing Co.

Design
Pentagram Design
Client
Flying Fish Brewing Co.

Design
Davies Hall
Client
Sainsbury's

(OPPOSITE PAGE)
Design
Tutssels
Client
Bass Brewers

Design
Creativstudio Mark & Neuosad
Client
Privatbrauerei Fritz Egger

Design
EJE Sociedad Publicitaria
Client
Bacardi Martini

Design
Poppe Tyson
Client
Penn Brewery

Design
Poppe Tyson
Client
Penn Brewery

(THIS PAGE)
Design
Landor Associates, London
Client
Del Haize

(OPPOSITE TOP)
Design
Hermsen Design Associates
Client
Rubinoff) Importing Co., Inc.

(OPPOSITE BOTTOM)
Design
Lewis Moberly
Client
Tesco

Design
Tucker Design
Client
The South Australian Brewing Co.

Design
Caldewey Design
Client
Staropramen Brewery

Design
Tutssels
Client
Tennent Caledonian Breweries

Design
Tieken Design and Creative Services
Client
Black Mountain Brewing Company

Design
Antista Fairclough Design
Client
Anheuser-Busch, Inc.

Design
Michael Peters Ltd.
Client
Fine Fare

Design
Kai Funck
Client
Holsten

Design
Nippon Design Center
Client
Asahi Breweries, Ltd.

Design
Nippon Design Center
Client
Asahi Breweries, Ltd.

Design
Hornall Anderson Design Works, Inc.
Client
Rhino Chasers

Design
Werkhaus Design
Client
Emerald City Brewing Co.

(OPPOSITE PAGE)
Design
Wickens Tutt Southgate
Client
Black Sheep Brewing Plc

Design
Hermsen Design Associates
Client
Rubinoff Importing Co., Inc.

(THIS PAGE)
Design
Taku Satoh Design Office Inc.
Client
Kirin Brewery Co. Limited

(This page)
Design
Christopher Hadden Design
Client
Shipyard Brewing Co.

(Opposite page)
Design
Bruce Hale Design
Client
August Schell Brewers

Design
Curtis Design
Client
The Stroh Brewery

Design
Leonhardt + Kern
Client
Schwaben Bräu Rob. Leicht KG

Design
Tucker Design
Client
Carlton & United Breweries

Design
Keith Harris Package Design
Client
Brauerei Frankenheim

Design
Antista Fairclough Design
Client
Anheuser-Busch, Inc.

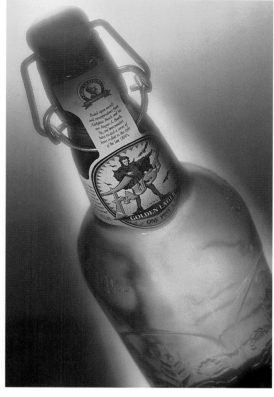

Design
Antista Fairclough Design
Client
Anheuser-Busch, Inc.

Design
Mark Oliver, Inc.
Client
Firestone Walker Brewing Co.

(THIS SPREAD)
Design
Cahan & Associates
Client
Boisset USA

Wine

WEIN

VIN

By John Grant and Barrie Tucker

BOTTLE DESIGN: FROM FUNCTION TO FASHION

Wine has long been regarded as the "social lubricant" of man. It has performed many a pivotal task during important moments in history—the Last Supper, the launching of great ships, and as for the Romans, well, no orgy has been complete without it. ■ *Despite its popularity and widespread consumption, wine has often been viewed as a relatively simple commodity with little or no perceived difference between one wine and another. With little requirement for branding, scant regard was paid to the way wine was presented. In what can only be described as an uninspired approach to wine packaging, the focus was all on function and naught on form. The bottle became the preferred container for wine primarily because it could easily store, maintain and transport wine, not because it looked good.* ■ *Today the story is vastly different, with the emphasis on artful presentation and the bottle sometimes serving as something like a handsome sculptural piece with the table top as the piazza. There are three main reasons for this change. First, wine is now a complex product differentiated by variety, region or country with a corresponding need for strong branding. Second, globalisation of the industry has seen increased competition in all markets with nearly 100,000 brands available worldwide. And third, consumers' attitudes toward wine have changed; the focus has moved from mere function to fashion. Today, a bottle must be designed not only to attract attention and encourage sale at the point of purchase, but it should also be attractive at the "point of consumption," that is, at home or in a restaurant. In addition to being a drink, for many consumers wine has*

(PREVIOUS SPREAD) DESIGN: DAVID LANCASHIRE DESIGN. CLIENT: BERRI RENMARO WINES. ■ (OPPOSITE PAGE) BARRIE TUCKER. PHOTO: STEVE KEOUGH.

JOHN GRANT IS EXECUTIVE GENERAL MANAGER OF MARKETING FOR SOUTHCORP WINES, AUSTRALIA'S LARGEST WINE PRODUCER. HE HAS SPENT THE LAST SIXTEEN YEARS IN THE LIQUOR INDUSTRY AND IS RESPONSIBLE FOR THE GLOBAL MARKETING OF SOUTHCORP WINES TO MORE THAN FIFTY COUNTRIES. ■ **BARRIE TUCKER** IS PRINCIPAL OF TUCKER DESIGN IN ADELAIDE, SOUTH AUSTRALIA. A MEMBER OF ALLIANCE GRAPHIQUE INTERNATIONALE AND THE DESIGN INSTITUTE OF AUSTRALIA, TUCKER IS INTERNATIONALLY RECOGNIZED FOR HIS WINE AND LIQUOR PACKAGING. HIS WORK HAS BEEN HONORED BY THE AUSTRALIAN GRAPHIC DESIGN ASSOCIATION AND HAS RECEIVED GOLD AND SILVER CLIO AWARDS.

become a statement of personal style. More than ever before, people are asking the question, "What does my choice in wine say about me?" ■ In today's crowded marketplace, wine marketers have to find ways of developing and conveying a "personality" for each brand. In the face of this challenge, wine marketers have quite literally turned to the bottle! ■ With 85 percent of wine consumed within 24 hours of purchase, there is no denying that the choice of a wine is often a last-minute decision based on use and price but also on appearance and whether or not the product's look suits the "mood" of the occasion and consumer's style. ■ Throughout the past five years, wine marketers—particularly in the USA, Australia and New Zealand—have focused on wine packaging. The results speak for themselves. One example is the transformation of the Seppelt brand. For 145 years Seppelt has been making award-winning sherries, Tokays, ports and muscats. However, the Seppelt brand was viewed as old-fashioned and was therefore slowly "dying on the vine." ■ By repackaging the range into slim-line "olive oil" bottles, some with etched labels, Seppelt has been successfully repositioned as an innovative, modern wine that appeals to the fashion-conscious, contemporary wine consumer. In the last financial year, sales of Seppelt sherry products increased 63 percent over the previous year. And dessert wines, like Tokay and muscat, have also experienced record increases. ■ Glass Mountain, a new product in the Seaview range released in early 1996, is a case in point. The unique frosted bottle and three-dimensional label has already won design awards and achieved sales of 100,000 cases within the first twelve months. Anecdotes filtering back from retailers tell tales of consumers responding instantly to the "cool, refreshing" look of the frosted bottle on a hot summer day. ■ A New Zealand producer last year appeared to break one of the major rules by releasing a new label in a royal blue bottle, a colour that has long been avoided because of its traditional connections with kerosene. Gaining controversial media coverage may not have been the only intention of the makers, but it has certainly resulted in a lot of publicity for the brand. ■ New bottle shapes and colours, new shapes and finishes to the top of bottles, exciting capsule and "no capsule" presentations, coloured synthetic closures replacing corks, ceramic printing onto glass, transparent labels and glass etching finishes are all being designed. ■ Whilst the world's winemakers may not like to believe it, the bottle has become just as important as the contents for many consumers when they are making a purchase. In the words of one Australian wine journalist: "To me presentation is everything. If the bottle looks exciting, colourful and interesting, then the chances are I'll have the cork out faster than you can say Barossa Valley."

«FLASCHENGESTALTUNG – VOM FUNKTIONALEN ZUM TRENDARTIKEL»
von John Grant and Barrie Tucker

Lange Zeit galt das Weintrinken als sozialer Akt. In wichtigen Augenblicken der Geschichte kam ihm eine zentrale Bedeutung zu – beim Abendmahl, bei Schiffstaufen (in Form von Champagner) und im alten Rom, wo eine Orgie ohne Wein nicht auszudenken war. Trotz seiner Beliebtheit bei breiten Schichten ist Wein in früheren Zeiten allgemein als relativ einfaches Getränk betrachtet worden, wobei eine Sorte kaum von der anderen zu unterscheiden war. Eine besondere Kennzeichnung durch Marken war kaum nötig, und deshalb wurde auch der gesamten Verpackung wenig Aufmerksamkeit geschenkt. Bei dieser Einstellung zur Verpackung, die man nur als «lustlos» bezeichnen kann, war alles auf Funktion und nicht auf Form ausgerichtet. Die Flasche wurde aus praktischen Gründen zum bevorzugten Behälter für Wein, vor allem weil sie einfach zu lagern und transportieren war, nicht weil sie gut aussah. ■ Heute sieht die Geschichte ganz anders aus: Die kunstvolle Präsentation steht im Vordergrund, und die Flasche kommt manchmal einer Skulptur gleich, die auf dem Tisch statt auf einer Piazza steht. Für diese Veränderung gibt es vor allem drei Gründe: Erstens ist Wein heute ein komplexes Produkt, das sich durch die Sorte, Region oder das Land unterscheidet, so dass eine eindeutige Kennzeichnung notwendig geworden ist. Zweitens hat die Globalisierung der Branche zu verstärkter Konkurrenz in allen Märkten geführt: weltweit gibt es 100'000 verschiedene Marken. Und drittens hat sich die Haltung der Konsumenten verändert: Wein ist ein Modegetränk geworden. Heute muss eine Flasche so gestaltet sein, dass sie nicht nur die Aufmerksamkeit auf sich zieht und am 'Ort des Verkaufs' zum Kauf lockt, sondern sie soll auch am 'Ort des Verbrauchs', das heisst zu Hause oder im Restaurant, attraktiv wirken. Für viele Konsumenten ist Wein nicht nur ein Getränk, sondern auch Ausdruck des persönlichen Stils. Mehr denn je fragen sich die Leute, was die Wahl des Weins über sie selbst verrät. ■ Das inzwischen riesige Angebot hat dazu geführt, dass die Marketing-Leute heute für jede Weinmarke eine «Persönlichkeit» entwickeln und sie dem Verbraucher vermitteln müssen. Angesichts dieser Herausforderung haben sie im wahrsten Sinne des Wortes zur Flasche gegriffen. ■ Da 85% der gekauften Weine innerhalb von 24 Stunden nach dem Kauf konsumiert werden, kann man nicht übersehen, dass die Wahl des Weins oft eine Entscheidung in letzter Minute ist, die vom Anlass und Preis abhängt, aber auch vom Aussehen und davon, ob das Äussere dem Anlass und oder dem Stil des Konsumenten entspricht. ■ In den letzten fünf Jahren haben die Wein-Vermarkter – besonders in den USA, Australien und Neuseeland – sich auf die Präsentation des Weines konzentriert. Die Resultate sprechen für sich. Als Beispiel sei die Seppelt-Marke erwähnt. Seit 145 Jahren hat Seppelt Prädikat-Sherries, Tokaierweine, Port- und Muskatweine produziert. Seppelt wirkte allmählich etwas verstaubt und verlor langsam an Boden. ■ Neue schlanke Flaschen, wie man sie oft für italienisches Olivenöl verwendet, zum Teil mit Etiketten in Kupferdruck, veränderten das Image erfolgreich: das Sortiment wirkte jetzt modern und sprach den modernen Weintrinker an. Im letzten Geschäftsjahr sind die Verkäufe der Sherries von Seppelt gegenüber dem Vorjahr um 63% gestiegen. Und der Absatz der Dessertweine wie Tokaier- und Muskatwein ist um phantastische 1'400% gestiegen, ein Rekordergebnis, das nicht so schnell zu schlagen sein wird. ■ Glass Mountain, ein neues Produkt im Seaview-Sortiment, das Anfang 1996 auf den Markt kam, ist ein

JOHN GRANT IST MARKETING-LEITER BEI SOUTHCORP WINES, DEM GRÖSSTEN WEINPRODUZENTEN AUSTRALIENS. ER HAT DIE LETZTEN SECHZEHN JAHRE IN DER ALKOHOL-BRANCHE GEARBEITET UND IST BEI SOUTHCORP FÜR DAS MARKETING DER WEINE IN ÜBER FÜNFZIG LÄNDERN ZUSTÄNDIG. ■ BARRIE TUCKER LEITET TUCKER DESIGN IN SÜDAUSTRALIEN. ER IST MITGLIED DER AGI UND DES DESIGN INSTITUTE OF AUSTRALIA. MIT DER GESTALTUNG VON FLASCHEN HAT ER INTERNATIONAL EINEN RUF ERWORBEN. SEINE ARBEITEN WURDEN VON DER AUSTRALIAN GRAPHIC DESIGN ASSOCIATION SOWIE MIT GOLD UND SILBER BEI DEN CLIO-WETTBEWERBEN AUSGEZEICHNET.

weiteres Paradebeispiel. Die einzigartige Milchglas-Flasche und das dreidimensionale Etikett haben bereits acht Design-Preise erhalten und zu Verkäufen von 100'000 Kisten in den ersten 12 Monaten geführt. Die Weinhändler berichten von Konsumenten, die an einem heissen Sommertag sdem kühlen, erfrischenden Look der Flasche nicht widerstehen können. ■ Ein Produzent aus Neuseeland hat letztes Jahr eine der wichtigsten Regeln gebrochen, indem er eine neue Sorte in einer königsblauen Flasche herausbrachte, eine Farbe, die normalerweise vermieden wird, weil viele dabei sofort an Kerosin denken. Die Produzenten haben vielleicht nicht in erster Linie mit kontroversen Mediendiskussionen spekuliert, aber diese brachten der

Marke zweifellos eine Menge Publizität. ■ Neue Flaschenformen und Farben, neue Formen und Manschetten für die Flaschenhälse, aufregende Verschlüsse und «verschlusslose» Varianten, farbige, synthetische Verschlüsse statt Korken, Siebdruck auf Glas, transparente Etiketten und Glasätzungen - das alles gibt es jetzt. ■ Auch wenn die Weinproduzenten der Welt es ungern glauben werden, so ist die Flasche heute für viele Konsumenten beim Einkauf so wichtig wie der Inhalt. Ein australischer Weinjournalist schreibt in diesem Zusammenhang: «Für mich ist die Präsentation alles. Wenn die Flasche aufregend aussieht, farbig und interessant, habe ich den Korken schneller draussen als ich Barossa Valley sagen kann.»

«LA BOUTEILLE, AU-DELÀ DE LA FORME»
par John Grant and Barrie Tucker

Depuis toujours, boire du vin est un acte social. Servi en de nombreuses occasions, en particulier pour célébrer des événements marquants, le vin a une signification cruciale dans les représentations de la Cène ou les baptêmes de navires au vin de champagne. Sans oublier, bien sûr, les Romains, pour lesquels aucune orgie digne de ce nom n'aurait pu se concevoir sans ce nectar des dieux. ■ Malgré sa popularité, le vin fut longtemps considéré comme une boisson ordinaire, et les crus ne se différenciaient guère les uns des autres. Comme il n'y avait nul besoin de les distinguer par des dénominations ou des «marques», peu d'importance fut accordée aux contenants. Le conditionnement devait être fonctionnel, et l'esthétique ne figurait pas au rang des préoccupations de l'époque. Facile à entreposer et à transporter, la bouteille s'imposa alors tout naturellement pour son aspect pratique et non pour l'harmonie de ses formes. ■ Aujourd'hui, les choses sont tout autres: la présentation passe au premier plan, et les bouteilles s'apparentent parfois à de véritables sculptures trônant sur les tables d'apparat. Trois raisons majeures ont présidé à ce changement. Premièrement, le vin est devenu un produit complexe, qui se distingue par son cépage ainsi que par sa région ou son pays d'origine. Une dénomination précise est donc devenue nécessaire. Deuxièmement, la globalisation de l'industrie viticole a entraîné un durcissement de la concurrence sur tous les marchés: on dénombre ainsi plus de 100'000 vins de différentes provenances dans le monde entier. Et troisièmement, l'attitude des consommateurs a changé elle aussi: le vin est devenu une boisson très prisée. Aujourd'hui, une bouteille est conçue pour attirer l'attention sur le point de vente, mais aussi – et c'est nouveau – sur le lieu de dégustation, c'est-à-dire à la maison ou au restaurant. Pour nombre d'amateurs, le vin est bien plus qu'une simple boisson, il est l'expression d'un style de vie. Et les amateurs se demandent ce que le choix d'un vin dévoile de leur personnalité. ■ Face à la saturation du marché, les professionnels du marketing doivent créer et développer une «personnalité» pour chaque cru. Et c'est en tentant de relever ce défi qu'ils se sont découvert une véritable passion pour la bouteille! ■ 85% des vins étant consommés dans les 24 heures suivant l'achat, il apparaît clairement que le choix d'un vin relève souvent d'un acte spontané, déterminé en fonction de l'occasion et du prix, mais aussi de la présentation qui doit répondre à l'humeur du moment et au style du consommateur. ■ Au cours des cinq dernières années – en particulier aux

Etats-Unis, en Australie et en Nouvelle-Zélande, les distributeurs de vin se sont concentrés sur la présentation du produit. Les résultats parlent d'eux-mêmes. L'évolution de la marque Seppelt en est un bon exemple. Durant 145 ans, le nom Seppelt fut synonyme de vins fins – sherrys, vins de Tokay, portos et muscats –, régulièrement primés. Pourtant, la marque souffrait d'une image un peu poussiéreuse qui, contrairement aux vins, ne se bonifiait pas avec le temps. ■ De nouvelles bouteilles, fines et élégantes comme certaines bouteilles d'huile d'olive italienne, et de belles étiquettes permirent de revisiter l'image de la marque, désormais apte à séduire le consommateur de vin moderne. Les résultats ne se firent pas attendre: lors du dernier exercice comptable, les ventes des sherrys Seppelt affichaient une progression de 63% par rapport à l'année précédente. Quant aux vins de dessert tels le Tokay et les muscats, les ventes ont fait un bond de 1400%, un record qui ne devrait pas être battu de sitôt! ■ Glass Mountain, un nouveau produit Seaview lancé sur le marché début 1996, fait aussi figure de parangon. Sa bouteille unique en verre opalin et son étiquette tridimensionnelle lui ont déjà valu huit design awards tandis que 100'000 caisses furent vendues durant les douze premiers mois. Les négociants témoignent de l'impact de la bouteille qui, lors des chaudes journées d'été, séduit spontanément les clients par la fraîcheur de son verre givré. ■ L'année dernière, un producteur néo-zélandais bafoua une règle bien établie en proposant un nouveau produit dans une bouteille bleu roi, une couleur généralement associée au kérosène et jusqu'alors bannie pour les spiritueux. Si la controverse médiatique qui s'ensuivit ne répondit pas à l'intention première des concepteurs, cette publicité inattendue servit largement la marque. ■ Nouvelles formes, nouvelles couleurs, goulots étirés, allongés, capsules délirantes, fermetures aux couleurs vives où les matières synthétiques remplacent le traditionnel bouchon en liège, sériegraphies, étiquettes transparentes et verre gravé, on trouve désormais de tout pour tous les goûts. ■ Ainsi, même si les producteurs viticoles ont peine à le croire, pour le consommateur, la bouteille est, lors de l'achat, aussi importante que le contenu. En témoignent les propos d'un journaliste australien à ce sujet: «Pour moi, la présentation est capitale. Si les formes de la bouteille sont excitantes, si la couleur est belle, alors il me faut moins de temps pour la déboucher qu'il ne m'en faut pour dire Barossa Valley!»

(OPPOSITE PAGE) JOHN GRANT, EXECUTIVE GENERAL MANAGER OF MARKETING FOR SOUTHCORP WINES, AUSTRALIA'S LARGEST WINE PRODUCER.

JOHN GRANT EST DIRECTEUR GÉNÉRAL DU MARKETING DE SOUTHCORP WINES, PREMIER PRODUCTEUR DE VINS EN AUSTRALIE. FORT D'UNE EXPÉRIENCE DE 16 ANS DANS LA BRANCHE, IL EST RESPONSABLE DU MARKETING DES VINS DANS PLUS DE 50 PAYS. ■ BARRIE TUCKER EST DIRECTEUR DE TUCKER DESIGN, AUSTRALIE. IL EST MEMBRE DE L'AGI ET DU DESIGN INSTITUTE OF AUSTRALIA. SES RÉALISATIONS ONT ÉTÉ HONORÉES PAR LA AUSTRALIAN GRAPHIC DESIGN ASSOCIATION, ET IL A REMPORTÉ LES PRIX OR ET ARGENT LORS DES CONCOURS CLIO.

(OPPOSITE PAGE)
Design
Blackburn's Limited
Client
Orchid Drinks

Design
Tucker Design
Client
Orlando Wyndham

Design
Britton Design
Client
Viansa Winery

(TOP LEFT)
Design
Britton Design
Client
Ferrari-Carano

(TOP RIGHT AND BOTTOM ROW)
Design
Britton Design
Client
Viansa Winery

Design
David Lancashire Design
Client
Self-promotion

Design
David Lancashire Design
Client
Self-promotion

(*OPPOSITE PAGE*)
Design
Swieter Design
Client
Hinkle Vineyard

Design
HM+E Incorporated
Client
Grenville Printing

Design
Lewis Moberly
Client
Asda Stores

Design
Tucker Design
Client
Padthaway Estate

Design
Immagine Design
Client
Antiche Fattorie Fiorentine

Design
Barrie Tucker Design
Client
David Wynn Wine Company

Design
Market + Design Ltd.
Client
Tesco Stores Ltd.

PROSPERITY RED
SANTA YNEZ VALLEY
RED TABLE WINE
PRODUCED AND BOTTLED BY
FIRESTONE VINEYARD, LOS OLIVOS, CA.

Design
Mark Oliver, Inc.
Client
Firestone Vineyard

Design
Caldewey Design
Client
Goosecross Cellars

Design
Michael Manwaring
Client
Hanna Winery

Design
Dashwood Design
Client
Montana Wines

Design
Caldewey Design
Client
Fetzer Vineyards

Design
Kosaka Design
Client
Zaca Mesa

Design
Keizo Matsui & Associates
Client
Yagi Shizou-Bu

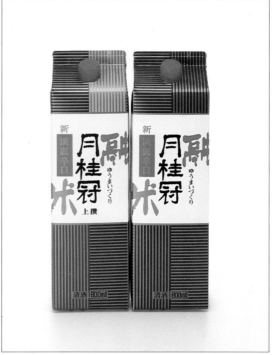

Design
Keizo Matsui & Associates
Client
Yagi Shizou-Bu

Design
TCD Corporation
Client
Hakutsuru Sake
Brewing Co., Ltd.

Design
Art 376, Penn State University

Design
Cato Design Inc.
Client
Vinefera Services Pty. Ltd.

Design
Antista Fairclough Design
Client
Heinz Weber

Wine

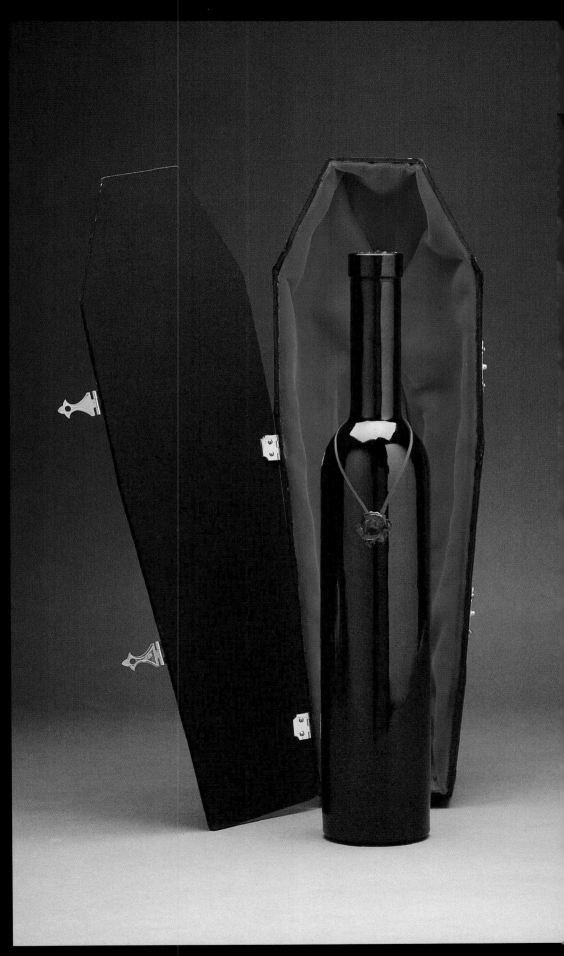

Design
Art 376, Penn State University
Client
Self-promotion

Wine

Design
Tucker Design
Client
Southcorp Wines

Design
Tucker Design
Client
Saddler's Creek Winery

Design
Tucker Design
Client
Saddler's Creek Winery

Design
Tucker Design
Client
Samuel Smith & Son P/L

Design
Tucker Design
Client
Southcorp Wines

Design
Tucker Design
Client
Samuel Smith & Son P/L

Design
Tucker Design
Client
Southcorp Wines

Design
Tucker Design
Client
Southcorp Wines

Design
Caldewey Design
Client
Boisset USA

Design
Blackburn's Limited
Client
Taylor, Fladgate & Yeatman

Design
Blackburn's Limited
Client
Allied Domecq

Design
Cato Design Inc.
Client
T'Gallant

Design
Cato Design Inc.
Client
T'Gallant

Design
Cato Design Inc.
Client
Stefano Lubiana Pty. Ltd.

Design
Cato Design Inc.
Client
Stefano Lubiana Pty. Ltd.

Design
Cato Design Inc.
Client
Mistwood

Design
Cato Design Inc.
Client
Hidden Creek

(BOTTOM ROW)
Design
Cato Design Inc.
Client
T'Gallant

(OPPOSITE PAGE)
Design
Cato Design Inc.
Client
T'Gallant

Design
Cato Design Inc.
Client
Peerick Vineyard

(THIS PAGE)
Design
W, G & R
Client
Marc-Etienne Dubois

(OPPOSITE PAGE)
Design
Art 376, Penn State University
Client
Self-promotion

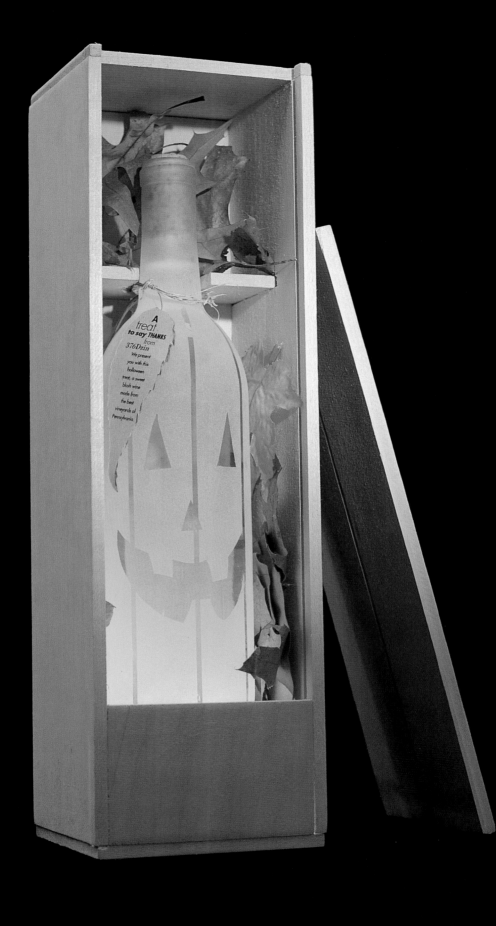

Design
Daedalos
Client
Golan Heights Winery

Design
David Lancashire Design
Client
Self-promotion

RED RED

THE BIBLE TELLS US "GO TO THE ANT,
CONSIDER HER WAYS AND BE WISE". WITH
THIS IN MIND WE RECOMMEND YOU GO TO
THE RED ANT RED AND ENJOY. MERRY
CHRISTMAS AND A PEACEFUL NEW YEAR TO
YOU AND YOURS FROM DAVID LANCASHIRE
DESIGN. RED-ANT RED WAS SPECIALLY
BOTTLED BY CAMPBELLS OF RUTHERGLEN.

1986
CABERNET

Design
David Lancashire Design
Client
Self-promotion

Design
Lewis Moberly
Client
Sogrape Vinhos de Portugal

Design
Pellegrini and Associates
Client
Pellegrini Vineyards

Design
Britton Design
Client
Viansa Winery

(OPPOSITE PAGE)
Design
Britton Design
Client
Galante Vineyards

GALANTE
VINEYARDS

RED ROSE HILL

1994 CARMEL VALLEY

Cabernet Sauvignon

ESTATE BOTTLED

ALC. 12.5% BY VOL.

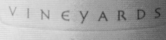

GALANTE
VINEYARDS

BLACKJACK PASTURE

1994 CARMEL VALLEY

Cabernet Sauvignon

ESTATE BOTTLED

ALC. 12.5% BY VOL.

Design
Caldewey Design
Client
Zia Cellars

Design
Lewis Moberly
Client
Sogrape Vinhos de Portugal

Design
Tangram Strategic Design
Client
Azienda Agriola Bulichella

Design
Supon Design Group
Client
Grand Palace Food International

Design
Primo Angeli Inc.
Client
Robert Mondavi Winery

Design
Lewis Moberly
Client
Asda

Design
Britton Design
Client
Opus One

Design
Britton Design
Client
Viansa Winery

Design
Caldewey Design
Client
Arbios Cellars

Design
Tharp Did It
Client
Mirassou Vineyards

Design
Tharp Did It
Client
Jory Winery

Design
Hixo
Client
Slaughter Leftwich

Design
Metzger & Metzger
Werbeagentur GmbH
Client
Fritz Croissant "Azienda
Agricola Vignano"

Design
Primo Angeli Inc.
Client
E & J Gallo Winery

Design
Hornall Anderson Design Works, Inc.
Client
Chateau Ste. Michelle Winery

Design
Buttgereit & Heidenrich
Client
Various & self-promotional

(OPPOSITE PAGE)
Design
Chateau La Nerthe
Client
in-house

FINE

CHÂTEAU
LA
NERTHE

CHATEAUNEUF-DU-PAPE

Spirits

SPIRITUOSEN

SPIRITUEUX

By Mary Lewis

MESSAGE ON THE BOTTLE

Maybe it's the fascination we have with the message in the bottle, so intriguing as it bobs along the waves, which fuels our interest in the message on the bottle. Perhaps it's our first experience of a vessel as a babe in arms. Or, it could be the buried relic, still intact, which holds many clues to the past. Whatever the reasons, bottles have their own special allure. Bottles have a narrative aura. They travel, they hold secrets and surprises. Dressed in their labels, their story becomes complete. Or does it? The contents still remain to be discovered... ■ From a packaging designer's perspective, bottle design is something apart—different from the cereals, detergents and nappies which typify our projects. In part this is because the bottle is not only a functional container, a carrier of a message and a competitive force, but it is also, importantly, often an object in its own right. It presents a broader brief, therefore, for the designer. ■ A tin of baked beans or a packet of crisps, no matter how perfect its design, is inevitably destined for the garbage. But a bottle, even when empty, may be cherished forever. Bottle designs for alcoholic beverages own the high ground in packaging. Exquisite cognac bottles sit happily alongside the most exquisite perfume bottles. Beer, wine and spirits belong to the category which brings packaging, perhaps the most commercial face of graphic design, closest to art. Mouton Rothschild and a host of New World wines have all played their part in this. ■ Most bottles are as much a reflection of one's personality as they are a practical container. The perfume bottles which grace a dressing table and the beverage bottles which languish in the cupboard

(PREVIOUS SPREAD) DESIGN: DUFFY DESIGN. CLIENT: JIM BEAM BRANDS. ■ (OPPOSITE PAGE) PORTRAIT OF MARY LEWIS. PHOTO BY JIM FORREST.

MARY LEWIS IS THE CREATIVE DIRECTOR OF LEWIS MOBERLY, A GRAPHIC DESIGN CONSULTANCY BASED IN LONDON. SHE AND HER PARTNER, ROBERT MOBERLY, FOUNDED THE AGENCY IN 1984. HER NUMEROUS INTERNATIONAL DESIGN AWARDS INCLUDE THE BRITISH DESIGN AND ART DIRECTION GOLD AWARD FOR OUTSTANDING DESIGN AND THE DESIGN BUSINESS ASSOCIATION DESIGN EFFECTIVENESS AWARDS GRAND PRIX. HER AWARD-WINNING PROJECTS INCLUDE THE IDENTITY AND PACKAGING DESIGN FOR UNITED DISTILLERS CLASSIC MALTS, DETTLING KIRSCHWASSER, ASDA, AND ZEISS LAGER.

speak volumes about their owners. So the bottle/label designer needs a highly tuned aesthetic which transcends function and form to pure image. ■ In my own work I am never happier than when I have a bottle to design. From the initial scribble to the final form, it is an exciting journey. I think of the bottle as a person, as a character possessing attitude and stance. In designing the label, I'm creating the clothes; in extending the range, I'm creating the family... ■ When I first designed bottles and labels in this category I noted that the labels which seemed "real" and to which one kept returning, were essentially "undesigned." The bare-faced simplicity and spontaneity of chalky writing on a port bottle, the intricate markings of a family crest, the slogans and slabs of mandatory text all have their own particular charm, especially when mixed together. Authenticity is usually a key criterion in this category. What makes a label authentic is its somewhat eclectic collection of graphics. ■ Brewers and distillers are usually family concerns. Each generation contributes to the label, and makes its own mark. When the clock stops, the result is somewhat *ad hoc* and, at the same time, surprisingly pleasing. ■ It is a real challenge for the designer to create from scratch. A successful bottle design will have focus, tension and pace. It will exude atmosphere and invite touch. People stroke bottles just like they twizzle their glass. ■ Technology (where are you without a widget?) and a proliferation of new products from "alcopops" to herbal blends have exploded onto the drink market. Many of these are aimed at the youth market. Most are short-lived because they either show their strategy or lack any heritage. ■ We have had a decade of overtly "marketed" products. Now, thankfully, a discerning consumer is looking for real values, real stories. ■ The joy of bottle design lies in the scope of the project—the process of weaving the story, sculpting the form and then creating the graphics. The order is not relevant, but the story is key. From this comes every nuance.

EINE FLASCHENBOTSCHAFT
von Mary Lewis

Vielleicht ist es die Faszination, die Neugier auf den Inhalt, die wir beim Anblick einer auf den Wellen schaukelnden Flaschenpost empfinden. ■ Vielleicht ist es die frühe Erfahrung einer Flasche als Schiff, die wir als Kleinkinder machten. ■ Oder es könnte eine vergrabene Reliquie sein, die, noch intakt, viele Hinweise auf die Vergangenheit enthält. Was auch immer, Flaschen haben ihren besonderen Reiz. ■ Flaschen haben etwas zu erzählen. Sie reisen, sie enthalten Geheimnisse und Überraschungen. Die Etiketten, mit denen sie geschmückt werden, erzählen die Geschichte zu Ende. Oder doch nicht? Der Inhalt bleibt noch immer zu entdecken... ■ Aus der Sicht eines Verpackungsdesigners ist Flaschengestaltung etwas Besonderes. Es ist anders als bei Getreideflocken, Waschmitteln und Windeln, mit denen wir es meistens zu tun haben. Das liegt zum Teil daran, dass die Flasche nicht nur ein funktioneller Behälter ist, Trägerin einer Botschaft und Instrument im Wettbewerb, sondern, und das ist wichtig, oft auch ein eigenständiges Objekt. Für den Designer bedeutet das eine umfassende Aufgabe. ■ Eine Konservendose für Bohnen oder eine Packung Chips landen unweigerlich im Abfall, auch wenn sie noch so gut gestaltet sind. Aber eine leere Flasche hebt man unter Umständen wegen ihrer Schönheit auf. Die Gestaltung von Flaschen für alkoholische Getränke gehört zum Anspruchsvollsten im Bereich des Packungsdesigns. Exquisite Cognac-Flaschen nehmen es ohne weiteres mit den exquisitesten Parfumflakons auf. ■ Verpackungen, vielleicht der kommerziellste Bereich des Graphik-Designs, kommen im Fall von Bier, Wein und Spirituosen der Kunst am nächsten. Mouton Rothschild und eine Menge Weine aus der Neuen Welt haben erheblich dazu beigetragen. ■ Die meisten Flaschen sind nicht nur praktische Behälter, sondern im gleichen Masse Ausdruck der Persönlichkeit. Die Parfumflakons auf einem Schminktisch und die Flaschen in der Vitrine sprechen Bände über ihre Besitzer. Der Gestalter von Flaschen und Etiketten braucht deshalb ein feines ästhetisches Empfinden, das sich über Form und Funktion hinaus auf das reine Bild erstreckt. ■ Ich selbst bin am glücklichsten bei der Arbeit, wenn ich eine Flasche gestalten kann. Von der ersten Skizze bis zur endgültigen Form ist es eine aufregende Reise. Ich betrachte eine Flasche als Person mit Charakter und einer bestimmten Haltung und Einstellung. Wenn ich das Etikett entwerfe, sind das ihre Kleider; wenn ich das Sortiment erweitere, schaffe ich die Familie.... ■ Als ich zum ersten Mal Flaschen und Etiketten in dieser Kategorie entwarf, stellte ich fest, dass die Etiketten, die «echt» wirkten und auf die man immer wieder zurückkam, jene waren, die nicht «gestylt» aussahen. Die Schlichtheit und Spontanität der Kreideschrift auf einer Flasche Portwein, die komplizierten Bestandteile eines Familienwappens, die obligatorischen Slogans und Texte haben alle ihren speziellen Charme, besonders wenn man sie vermischt. ■ Eigenständigkeit ist gewöhnlich ein Hauptkriterium in dieser Sparte. Und ein Etikett wirkt durch eine etwas eklektische Kombination von Graphik authentisch. ■ Brauereien und Brennereien sind meistens Familienbetriebe. Jede Generation hat etwas zum Etikett beigetragen, jede hat es zu ihrem eigenen, persönlichen Zeichen gemacht. Wenn die Uhr angehalten wird, ist das Ergebnis irgendwie zufällig und dabei überraschend ansprechend. Für einen Designer ist es eine echte Herausforderung, ein Etikett von Grund auf zu entwerfen. ■ Zu einer erfolgreichen Flasche gehört eine gezielte Ausrichtung, Spannung und Rhythmus. Sie schafft Atmosphäre und lädt zur Berührung ein. Die Leute streicheln Flaschen ebenso wie sie ihr Glas von allen Seiten betrachten. ■ Die Technologie und eine Unmenge neuer Produkte wie Mixgetränke und Kräuterversionen haben sich auf dem Getränkemarkt breit gemacht. Viele dieser Produkte richten sich an Jugendliche. Die meisten sind kurzlebig, weil die Strategie zu offensichtlich ist oder weil sie keine Tradition haben. ■ Wir haben ein Jahrzehnt hinter uns, in dem Produkte dominierten, die allein vom Marketing 'gepusht' wurden. Heute schaut der kritisch gewordene Konsument zum Glück auf echte Werte, echte Geschichten. ■ Die Freude an der Flaschengestaltung liegt im Umfang der Aufgabe – dem Verweben der Fäden zu einer Geschichte, in der Schaffung der Form und in der graphischen Gestaltung. Die Reihenfolge ist unbedeutend, aber die Geschichte ist der Schlüssel. Jede Nuance ergibt sich daraus.

MARY LEWIS IST CREATIVE DIRECTOR VON LEWIS MOBERLY, EINE GRAPHIK-DESIGNFIRMA IN LONDON. SIE UND IHR PARTNER ROBERT MOBERLY GRÜNDETEN DIE AGENTUR 1984. MARY HAT ZAHLREICHE INTERNATIONALE DESIGN-PREISE GEWONNEN, U.A. DEN BRITISH DESIGN AND ART DIRECTION GOLD AWARD FÜR HERVORRAGENDES DESIGN UND DEN GRAND PRIX DER DESIGN BUSINESS ASSOCIATION, DIE PREISE FÜR EFFEKTIVES, ERFOLGREICHES DESIGN VERGIBT. ZU DEN FÜR ERSCHEINUNGSBILD UND VERPACKUNG AUSGEZEICHNETEN PRODUKTEN, FÜR DIE SIE ZUSTÄNDIG WAR, GEHÖREN UNITED DISTILLERS CLASSIC MALTS, DETTLING KIRSCHWASSER, ASDA WINES AND SPIRITS SOWIE ZEISS-BIER.

HISTOIRE DE BOUTEILLES
par Mary Lewis

Peut-être est-ce cette fascination que nous éprouvons en voyant une bouteille à la mer ballottée par les vagues, le mystère qui entoure son message? ■ Peut-être est-ce ce petit bateau flottant et vacillant enfoui dans nos souvenirs d'enfance? ■ Ou peut-être est-ce cette relique, encore intacte, que nous avons religieusement conservée et qui renferme une page d'histoire? Peu importe la raison, chaque bouteille a son attrait particulier. ■ Les bouteilles ont une histoire à raconter: elles ont l'âme vagabonde, recèlent quantité de mystères et de surprises. Une histoire entièrement révélée par l'étiquette? Pas vraiment. L'histoire se savoure pleinement une fois le contenu en bouche. ■ Pour tout designer de packagings, donner forme à une bouteille est, en quelque sorte, un exercice de style. Rien à voir avec les céréales, les lessives et les couches-culottes pour bébés, le lot commun des designers. Car la bouteille ne se réduit pas à un contenant, qui délivre un message ou incite à l'achat. C'est un objet à part entière! Et c'est ce qui fait toute la différence. D'où l'importance de la tâche pour le designer. ■ Une conserve de haricots ou un paquet de chips terminera immanquablement sa course dans une poubelle. Mais une bouteille, même vide, sera peut-être conservée éternellement. Dans le domaine du packaging, la création de bouteilles tient indubitablement le haut du pavé. Les plus belles bouteilles de cognac ne rivalisent-elles pas avec les plus beaux flacons de parfum? ■ Le conditionnement – peut-être le domaine le plus commercial du design graphique – se rapproche le plus de l'art lorsqu'il se fait l'écrin du vin, de la bière et des spiritueux. Le Mouton Rothschild et moult autres grands crus ont largement contribué à lui donner ses lettres de noblesse. ■ Nombre de bouteilles vont au-delà de leur aspect fonctionnel, devenant le miroir de la personnalité. Les flacons de parfum qui ornent une coiffeuse et les bouteilles qui trônent derrière une vitrine nous tiennent le même langage, dévoilant les facettes de leur propriétaire. C'est pourquoi tout designer de bouteilles et d'étiquettes doit avoir un sens aigu de l'esthétique qui transcende forme et fonction pour arriver à une image pure. ■ Dans mon travail, ma plus grande joie est de donner corps à une bouteille. De la première ébauche à la forme définitive, c'est un voyage excitant. A mes yeux, une bouteille, c'est comme une personne: elle possède un caractère et une attitude qui lui sont propres. Lorsque je dessine l'étiquette, je l'habille, lorsque j'élargis l'assortiment, je crée une famille. ■ En faisant mes premières armes dans ce domaine, je me suis rendu compte que les «vraies» étiquettes, celles auxquelles on demeure fidèle, n'étaient pas «stylisées». La simplicité et la spontanéité de quelques lettres tracées à la craie sur une bouteille de porto, les éléments complexes des armoiries d'une famille, les appellations et autres indications présentent toutes un attrait particulier, encore renforcé par leur réunion. Ici, l'authenticité constitue un critère clé. Et l'authenticité réside justement dans cette combinaison graphique éclectique. ■ Les brasseries et distilleries sont souvent des entreprises familiales. Chaque génération a imprimé sa marque à l'étiquette. A un moment, le temps s'est arrêté, le temps de laisser son empreinte personnelle, et le résultat, surprenant, est souvent dans le ton, séduisant. Pour un designer, créer une étiquette en partant de rien constitue un véritable défi. ■ Une bouteille réussie suit une ligne et un objectif précis, allie rythme et tension. Elle crée une atmosphère, on a envie de la toucher. Les gens caressent une bouteille comme ils scrutent un verre. ■ La technologie et une quantité de nouveaux produits, comme les mix et les versions aromatisées, ont envahi le marché. La plupart s'adressent aux jeunes et ont une durée de vie relativement courte, soit parce que la stratégie est trop évidente, soit parce que la tradition fait défaut. ■ Au cours de la dernière décennie, le succès d'une boisson relevait entièrement de la stratégie marketing. Aujourd'hui, les consommateurs, plus critiques, recherchent aussi de vraies valeurs, de vraies histoires. ■ Le plaisir de créer une bouteille réside dans l'envergure de la tâche – tisser une histoire, sculpter une forme, donner une identité graphique. Peu importe dans quel ordre on procède, l'essentiel, c'est l'histoire. Et c'est de là que vient chaque nuance.

MARY LEWIS OCCUPE LE POSTE DE DIRECTRICE DE CRÉATION CHEZ LEWIS MOBERLY, UNE AGENCE DE DESIGN GRAPHIQUE BASÉE À LONDRES QU'ELLE FONDA EN 1984 AVEC SON ASSOCIÉ ROBERT MOBERLY. ELLE A REMPORTÉ DE NOMBREUX PRIX DE DESIGN INTERNATIONAUX, DONT LE BRITISH DESIGN AND ART DIRECTION GOLD AWARD ET LE GRAND PRIX DÉCERNÉ PAR LA DESIGN BUSINESS ASSOCIATION, QUI COURONNE QUALITÉ ET EFFICACITÉ DU DESIGN. PARMI LES PRODUITS PRIMÉS POUR LEUR IDENTITÉ VISUELLE ET LEUR PACKAGING FIGURENT LES WHISKIES UNITED DISTILLERS CLASSIC, LE KIRSCH DETTLING, LES VINS ET LES SPIRITUEUX ASDA AINSI QUE LA BIÈRE ZEISS.

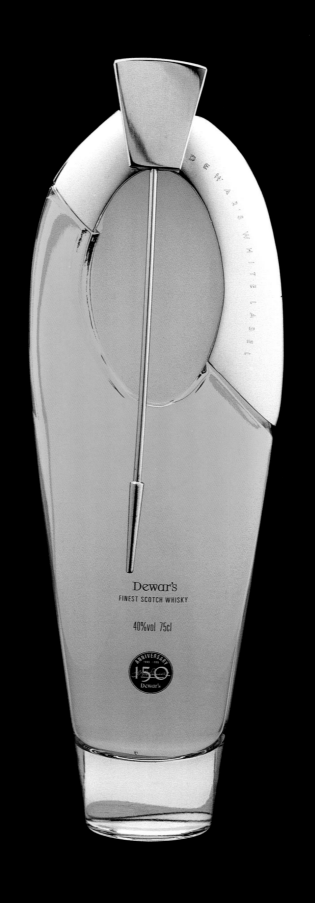

Dewar's
FINEST SCOTCH WHISKY

40%vol 75cl

Design
Tutssels
Client
United Distillers

Design
Taku Satoh Design Office Inc.
Client
Takara Shuzo Co., Ltd.

Design
Duffy Design
Client
Jim Beam Brands

Design
Duffy Design
Client
Jim Beam Brands

Design
Duffy Design
Client
Jim Beam Brands

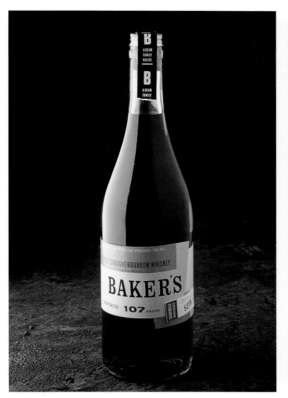

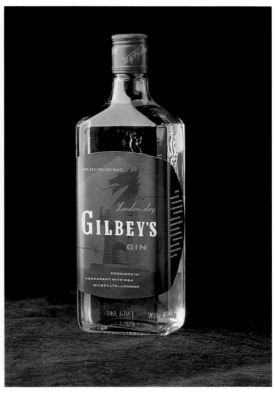

(THIS PAGE)
Design
Duffy Design
Client
Jim Beam Brands

Design
Duffy Design
Client
Jim Beam Brands

Design
Duffy Design
Client
Jim Beam Brands

Design
Charles S. Anderson Design Co.
Client
Distillerie de Aravis

Design
Nippon Design Center, Inc.
Client
The Nikka Whisky Distilling Co., Ltd.

Design
Thorburn Design
Client
Millenium

MERRY CHRISTMAS

Design
Tucker Design
Client

Design
Tucker Design
Client
Southcorp Wines

Design
Albert Zimmermann
Client
Self-promotion

Design
Claessens International London
Client
IDV

Design
Graphic Partners
Client
Glenturret Distillers

Design
Blackburn's Limited
Client
Berry Bros. & Rudd Ltd.

Design
Blackburn's Limited
Client
Berry Bros. & Rudd Ltd.

Design
Hundred Design Inc.
Client
Suntory Co., Ltd.

Design
Wickens Tutt Southgate
Client
Seagram UK Ltd.

Design
Michael Peters Ltd.
Client
Ballantine's

Design
Kollberg/Johnson Associates
Client
Austin Nichols

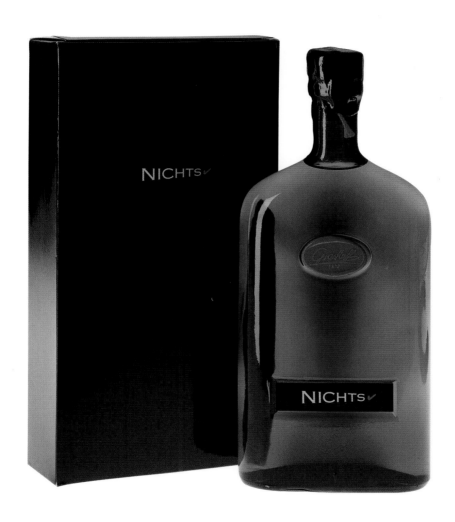

Design
Atelier Haase & Knels
Client
B. Grashoff Nachf.

(THIS SPREAD)
Design
Designers Company
Client
Hooghoudt Distillers BV

Design
Futura
Client
Dana Mirna

Design
Charles S. Anderson Design Co.
Client
Distillerie de Aravis

Design
Daedalus Design
Client
Societe Slaur

(OPPOSITE PAGE)

Design

Pearlfisher

Design
Duffy Design
Client
Jim Beam Brands

(Opposite page)
Design
K-Design
Client
Distillerie Studer

(THIS PAGE)
Design
Lewis Moberly
Client
Arnold Dettling

Design
Nippon Design Center
Client

Design
Daedalus Design
Client
Cognac Raymound Ragnaud

Design
George Lachaise Design
Client
Elie-Arnaud Denoix

Design
Baxmann & Harnickell
Client
H.C. Asmussen

Design
Klim Design
Client
Casa Cuervo, S.A. de C.V.

Design
Keith Harris Package Design
Client
I.B. Berentzen

Design
Keith Harris Package Design
Client
Lucas Bols

Design
Werkhaus Design
Client
Katahdin Brands

Design
Klim Design
Client
Casa Cuervo, S.A. de C.V.

Design
Lewis Moberly
Client
United Distillers

Design
Blackburn's Limited
Client
United Distillers

Design
Klim Design
Client
Casa Cuervo, S.A. de C.V.

Design
Sargent & Berman
Client
Osobya Marketing Group

Design
Graphic Partners
Client
Allied Domecq

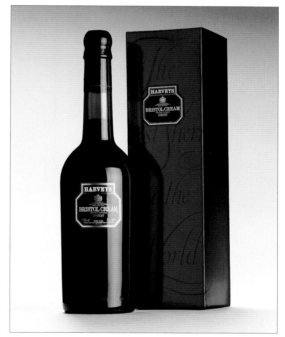

Design
Blackburn's Limited
Client
Highland Distilleries

Design
Blackburn's Limited
Client
Allied Domecq

Design
K-Design
Client
Distillerie Studer

Design
Charles S. Anderson Design Company
Client
Distillerie de Aravis

Design
Graphic Partners
Client
Glenturret Distillers

Design
Graphic Partners
Client
Allied Domecq

Design
Market + Design Ltd.
Client
The Gaymer Group Ltd.

Design
Designers Company
Client
Hooghoudt Distillers BV

Translations and Captions

ÜBERSETZUNGEN UND LEGENDEN

TRADUCTIONS ET LÉGENDES

von Véronique Vienne

EIN GESPRÄCH MIT MICHEL ROUX

Michel Roux, Direktor und Geschäftsführer von Carillon Importers, war der Hauptstratege der hochgelobten Werbekampagne für Absolut-Wodka. Über 15 Jahre hinweg sind über 500 Absolut-Anzeigen erschienen – mit einer aus zwei Worten bestehenden Headline unter dem Photo einer klaren Flasche schwedischen Wodkas. Man musste schon ein Illusionist sein, um eine schlichte, medizinisch wirkende Flasche mit kurzem Hals und abgerundeten Ecken zu einer unverwechselbaren Ikone einer ganzen Generation von Wodka-Trinkern zu machen. Michel Roux hat das geschafft. Ohne Frage ist er ein Marketing-Zauberer. «Michel (Ideen) zu präsentieren ist als präsentiere man vor Gott», sagt ein junger Media-Einkäufer, der für eine der anderen Werbekampagnen arbeitete.

Als Roux 1970 zu Carillon kam, war er ihr erster Verkäufer. Seitdem hat er die Firma in Teaneck, New Jersey, zu einem führenden Importeur von Spirituosen gemacht – zu einem Grossisten, der einige der berühmtesten europäischen Markennamen in dem Bereich, u.a. Stolichnaya, Grand Marnier und Bombay, anbietet. Ironischerweise vertreibt Carillon Absolut, die Marke, die sie berühmt gemacht haben, nicht mehr. 1993 übergab der schwedische Eigentümer von Absolut den Account Seagram, was selbst Insider der New Yorker Werbeszene überraschte. Zum selben Zeitpunkt bekam Carillon Stolichnaya, einen erstklassigen russischen Wodka. Dieser plötzliche Wechsel war für Roux eine Herausforderung. Jeder fragte sich, ob er sich wohl mit einer Marke anfreunden könne, die Absoluts Erzrivale gewesen war. Kein Problem. Einmal Jongleur, immer Jongleur. Michel Roux beschwor seine Geister und machte sich an die Arbeit. Heute ist der russische Wodka dabei, die an den schwedischen Konkurrenten verlorenen Marktanteile zurückzugewinnen.

VV: Ich habe gehört, dass Sie in Frankreich, in der Region Poiton- Charentes, nicht weit von Cognac, geboren wurden.

MR: In diesem Teil von Frankreich liegt nichts weit entfernt von einander.

VV: Die Franzosen trinken gern, besonders in dieser Region. Versuchen Sie, den amerikanischen Konsumenten die Trinkkultur Ihrer Heimat zu vermitteln?

MR: Nein, auf keinen Fall, der Unterschied ist zu gross. Wo ich herkomme, sitzt man 10 bis 20 Minuten vor einem Glas Wein. Die Franzosen nippen am Glas. Die Amerikaner dagegen trinken Alkohol sehr schnell, sie spülen den Inhalt ihres Glases herunter, um schnell in Stimmung zu kommen.

VV: Bevor Sie zu Carillon kamen, haben Sie Nachtclubs und Restaurants in Texas geführt. Das muss am Anfang ein Kulturschock gewesen sein.

MR: In dieser Zeit habe ich gelernt, dass die Verpackung einer Flasche genau so wichtig ist wie ihr Inhalt. Während sich die Franzosen wenig aus der Flasche selbst machen, sind die Amerikaner visuell orientierte Trinker.

VV: Aber da ist noch der mentale, emotionale und gesellschaftliche Faktor, der mit einer Flasche verbunden ist, in anderen Worten, die Marke. Ich glaube, das ist wirklich Ihre Spezialität.

MR: Das stimmt. Die Marke ist etwas, das mit allen Sinnen wahrgenommen wird. Aber zuerst das Wichtigste: wenn die Verpackung anspricht, sind die Leute eher bereit, auch den Inhalt gut zu finden.

VV: Was macht eine Verpackung ansprechend?

MR: Sie muss faszinierend sein – vom Etikett bis zur Form der Flasche und der Farbe des Getränks. Als wir uns z.B. mit der blauen Flasche für Bombay-Gin befassten, sagten uns die Marktforschungsleute, dass die farbige Flasche den Gin wie Mundwasser aussehen liesse. Mundwasser? Bestimmt nicht! Vielleicht wie ein Parfum, aber sicher nicht wie Mundwasser. Tatsächlich nehmen sich heute viele Parfumflaschen-Designer Flaschen für Spirituosen zum Vorbild und auch umgekehrt.

VV: Sie haben recht. Die Flaschen für Calvin Kleins «cK One», Hilfigers «Tommy» und Perry Ellis' «America» ähneln Rum- bzw. Wodkaflaschen. Oder nehmen wir das Parfum «Champagne» von Yves Saint Laurent. Vielleicht gibt es eine Erklärung dafür. Ich habe einmal gelesen, dass Kölnisch Wasser aus einer Mischung von Grappa (Traubenschnaps) und essentiellen Ölen hergestellt wurde. Es konnte als Schnaps getrunken oder als Parfum verwendet werden.

MR: Zu Hause in der Provence stelle ich Wodka mit Lavendel aus meinem Garten her. Er riecht so gut, dass man sich am liebsten damit einreiben möchte. Wussten Sie übrigens, dass Andy Warhol Absolut-Wodka als Parfum benutzte? Es war *sein* Parfum. Ich weiss nicht, ob er den Geruch mochte oder ob er zu geizig war, ein richtiges Parfum zu kaufen. Aber erwähnen Sie das lieber nicht, sonst meinen einige Leser vielleicht, dass wir es gut finden, wenn jemand nach Gin riecht und Parfum trinkt!

VV: Haben Sie Pläne in Richtung einer Vermarktung Ihres eigenen Lavendel-Wodkas?

MR: Eher nicht. Ich habe alle Hände voll damit zu tun, Carillons Marken zu vermarkten. Marketing ist wie Gärtnern: Wenn man zu viele Gemüse zu nah beieinander pflanzt, haben sie zu wenig Platz, und keines wird gut kommen. Eine Marke aufzubauen dauert Jahre. Und man braucht ausserdem Geduld. Manchmal tut man gar nicht so viel. Manchmal ist es am besten, die Flasche oder die Verpackung so zu lassen, wie sie ist. Wenn man ein alteingesessenes Produkt hat, muss man mit Veränderungen sehr behutsam sein. Beim Grand Marnier zum Beispiel haben wir einen Teil des Etiketts ein bisschen modernisiert, aber wir liessen die Flasche wie sie ist – sie war ganz einfach der Inbegriff von Qualität.

VV: Was machen Sie genau? Wie zum Beispiel schaffen Sie es, ein Produkt, das typisch schwedisch oder französisch ist, zu einem Teil der amerikanischen Kultur zu machen?

MR: Am schwersten ist es, den Herstellern klar zu machen, wie ihr Produkt in einem anderen Land wirkt. Zum Beispiel war es fast unmöglich, den Stolichnaya-Leuten zu erklären, warum sie ihr Sortiment mit einem aromatisierten Wodka erweitern sollten. Gefühlsmässig waren sie gegen die Idee. Für sie war es ein Sakrileg. Es war, als würde ich meinem französischen Kunden erzählen, sein Rotwein Château de Beaulieu müsse im Eisschrank gelagert und gekühlt serviert werden.

VV: Ihre Aufgabe ist es also, herumzureisen, und jedem den amerikanischen Lebensstil zu erklären?

MR: So ist es, genau das tue ich. Es ist ein undankbarer Kreuzzug. Der Erfolg einer Marke hängt davon ab, wie gut ich den Leuten erklären kann, wie ihr Produkt in den USA empfunden wird. Manchmal muss ich nicht viel sagen, aber manchmal muss ich einige Male hin- und herreisen.

VV: Reisen Sie viel?

MR: Nach Frankreich und England sechs bis sieben Mal pro Jahr, nach Russland fast jeden Monat.

VV: Wie sieht Ihre Marktforschung aus?

MR: Meine Methode besteht darin, dass ich selbst herausfinde, was läuft, und zwar an Ort und Stelle. Das ist nicht sehr anspruchsvoll, aber es funktioniert. Um eine Marke aufzubauen, muss man selbst die Psyche der Konsumenten verstehen. Ich spreche zum Beispiel mit Barkeepern und trinke mit ihnen. In französischen Spirituosen- Firmen muss das Aussendienstpersonal einmal im Jahr eine Entziehungskur machen, weil ihr Job bedingt, dass sie mit Barkeepern und mit ihren Kumpeln trinken. Bevor sie sich versehen, haben sie fünfzehn Drinks intus. Hier in Amerika ist es ein bisschen einfacher, ein Beziehungsnetz aufzubauen: man kann mogeln, indem man sein Glas heimlich in einen Gummibaumtopf leert!

VV: Machen sie auch traditionelle Marktforschung mit Zielgruppen und Umfragen?

MR: Ja. Soweit ich das beurteilen kann, ist das alles für die Katz –, aber wir machen es trotzdem.

VV: Was sieht zum Beispiel der typische Stolichnaya-Trinker aus?

MR: Es gibt zwei verschiedene Tpyen: der eine trinkt Stoli und der andere aromatisierten Stoli. Der eine ist 35 Jahre alt und älter, der andere ist jünger, so zwischen 21 und 40. Der reine Stoli ist für Männer gedacht, der aromatisierte für Frauen. Das ist natürlich Theorie. Ich glaube, dass sich im Leben alles irgendwann herauskristallisiert – ob wir es nun steuern oder nicht. Wir haben auf Trends so gut wie keinen Einfluss. Früher zum Beispiel schauten junge Leute auf die älteren, um zu sehen, was diese trinken - heute ist es umgekehrt. Ältere Leute eifern den Jüngeren nach. Ausserdem fühlt sich heute mit 50 oder 60 niemand mehr alt. Es ist deshalb schwer, eine Zielgruppe zu definieren. Wer bin ich denn, dass ich einen Mann davon abbringe, einen Drink zu bestellen, der eigentlich für Frauen gedacht ist? Ich glaube, dass alle näher zusammenrücken, jung und alt, Männer und Frauen.

VV: Was macht denn einen guten Marketing-Mann aus?

MR: Instinkt. Ich habe nie eine Marketing-Schule besucht, aber ich weiss, was der Durchschnittsbürger will, wobei er entspannen kann und was er bereit ist zu kaufen, um sich wohl zu fühlen. Ich erkenne das Potential von Dingen. Übrigens hat die Vermarktung von Alkohol nicht unbedingt etwas mit Trinken zu tun - Gott sei Dank. Bei Absolut-Wodka zum Beispiel verbanden wir die Marke mit gesellschaftlichem Beisammensein und Mode, weil das zu dieser Zeit genau das war, wobei sich die Leute gut fühlten.

VV: Was halten Sie heute von der Absolut-Kampagne?

MR: Für die Flasche war ich nicht zuständig, ich habe nur das Image aufgebaut. Und das nicht alleine. Es waren viele Leute involviert – die meisten von ihnen versuchen heute, den Erfolg der Kampagne auf ihr Konto zu buchen. Mir ist das egal.

VV: Eine Ihrer grössten Marken ist jetzt Stolichnaya – was haben Sie vor?

MR: Die Stolichnaya-Flasche ist nicht gerade umwerfend. Wenn man sich das Etikett wegdenkt, bleibt nicht viel. Sie sieht fast so aus wie jede andere Flasche mit gewöhnlichem russischen Wodka. Das ist nicht unbedingt schlecht. Im Cognac-Gebiet zum Beispiel sind aufgemotzte Flaschen für erstklassige Cognacs out und schlichte Flaschen in. Schlichtheit wird als erstklassig betrachtet. Die Stoli-Flasche hat nicht viel zu bieten, aber das Etikett ist aussergewöhnlich – es lässt den Inhalt nach etwas Besonderem aussehen. Und natürlich trägt die Werbekampagne unter dem Slogan "Freedom of Vodka" mit den Bildern der russischen Avantgarde-Künstler zum Gefühl der Authenzität und Einzigartigkeit bei.

VV: Kann eine Marke, die nicht beworben wird, wachsen?

MR: Nachdem sie eine bestimmte Ebene erreicht hat, hört sie auf zu wachsen. Die Rolle der Werbung ist es, bei den Verbrauchern ein Gefühl von Wohlbefinden zu fördern. Aber eine Marke, für die geworben wird, muss auch durch Mundpropaganda gestützt werden. Eine Marke aufzubauen ist ein unendlicher Prozess – man bearbeitet Bar für Bar, eine nach der anderen.

VV: Sie sprechen mit Barkeepern, und die wiederum sprechen mit den Gästen?

MR: Man spricht nicht nur mit den Barkeepern, sondern man mischt sich auch unter ihre Gäste. Man muss schon angefressen genug sein von einer Marke, um sie Abend für Abend zu trinken.

VV: Sind Sie eine Werbemaschine für Ihre Marken?

MR: Das könnte man so ausdrücken. Obwohl ich seit kurzem versuche, ein wenig zu reduzieren.

VV: Woher nehmen Sie die Energie, Nacht für Nacht auszugehen?

MR: Es ist ein bisschen wie Sex im Alter von siebzig Jahren. Aber die Tatsache, dass ich meine Marken mag, motiviert mich, und ich möchte, dass jeder sie so schätzt wie ich. In unserer Firma wird jeder zum Botschafter für unsere Produkte. So einfach ist das. Vor Jahren, als ich an der Absolut-Kampagne arbeitete, besuchte ich eines Abends Freunde in ihrem Haus auf den Hamptons. Kaum war ich drinnen, servierten sie Stolichnaya. Ich drehte mich auf dem Absatz um und ging. Ich konnte es nicht ertragen, dass sie das Konkurrenzprodukt tranken. Eine Marke aufzubauen heisst, sie zu leben. Ich weiss nicht, warum die Leute das manchmal nicht begreifen.

VV: Für Sie ist der Aufbau einer Marke wie das Bestellen eines Gartens, nicht wahr?

MR: Ja, für mich schon. Ich bin auf dem Lande geboren, und ich bin ein Naturmensch. Jeden Morgen schaue ich nach, was mein Salat, meine Erdbeeren und meine Kartoffeln machen – ich schaue nach meinen Marken, wie ein Bauer nach seinen Feldern schaut. Ich will, dass etwas wächst, und muss mich jeden Tag darum kümmern. Es geht ums Hegen und Pflegen: eine Marke ist kein totes Objekt, sie reagiert auf die Fürsorge, die sie erhält. Mir gefällt diese Zeile von dem französischen Dichter Alphonse de Lamartine: Objets inanimés, avez-vous donc une âme / qui s'attache à notre âme et la force d'aimer? (Ihr leblosen Objekte, habt ihr also eine Seele / die sich an unsere Seele bindet und sie zwingt zu lieben?) Ich kann Ihnen sagen, dieses Geschäft hat nichts mit dem Konsum von Alkohol zu tun, sondern damit, dass man an etwas glaubt und dafür lebt.

MICHEL ROUX IST PRÄSIDENT UND GESCHÄFTSFÜHRER VON CARILLON IMPORTERS. ER WAR WESENTLICH AN DER ENTWICKLUNG, DEM VERTRIEB UND DEM ERFOLG VIELER EUROPÄISCHER PRODUKTE IN DEN USA BETEILIGT, U.A. VON STOLICHNAYA WODKA, GRAND MARNIER, ABSOLUT WODKA, BOMBAY GIN, UND PERLE DE BRILLET. ROUX HAT SICH ALS AUSSERGEWÖHNLICHER MARKETING-EXPERTE SOWIE AUCH ALS PHILANTHROP, KUNSTFREUND UND ENGAGIERTER BÜRGER EINEN NAMEN GEMACHT. ER IST FÜR SEINE GESCHÄFTLICHEN UND SOZIALEN AKTIVITÄTEN MEHRFACH AUSGEZEICHNET WORDEN.

VÉRONIQUE VIENNE LEBT UND ARBEITET ALS AUTORIN IN BROOKLYN, NEW YORK. SIE IST IN PARIS GEBOREN UND AUFGEWACHSEN UND HAT AN DER ECOLE DES BEAUX-ARTS ARCHITEKTUR STUDIERT. NACHDEM SIE MEHRERE JAHRE ALS AUSSTELLUNGSGESTALTERIN GEARBEITET HATTE, WURDE SIE ART DIREKTORIN BEI ZEITSCHRIFTEN WIE INTERIORS, PARENTING UND SELF. HEUTE SCHREIBT SIE FÜR VERSCHIEDENE PUBLIKATIONEN ÜBER DESIGN UND KULTURELLE TRENDS.

UNE INTERVIEW AVEC MICHEL ROUX

Michel Roux, P.-D.G. de Carillon Importers, fut le principal stratège de la célèbre campagne Absolut Vodka. Pendant 15 ans, plus de 500 visuels ont illustré la bouteille de vodka suédoise. La création de cet icone sophistiqué, caractéristique de toute une génération d'amateurs de vodka, à partir d'une simple fiole à l'allure médicinale, au col court et aux formes arrondies, relevait de l'illusionnisme. Un talent dont Michel Roux peut se prévaloir. Tout le monde s'entend en effet pour qualifier cet homme de magicien du marketing: «Présenter des idées à Michel, c'est comme les présenter à Dieu!», déclare un jeune acheteur publicitaire qui a travaillé pour l'une de ses campagnes.

A ses débuts chez Carillon en 1970, Roux était le premier vendeur. Depuis, il a fait de l'entreprise de Teaneck, New Jersey, l'un des principaux importateurs de spiritueux distribuant quelques-unes des plus fameuses marques européennes dont Stolichnaya, Grand Marnier et Bombay. L'ironie du sort veut qu'aujourd'hui, Carillon ne vende plus Absolut, le produit qui l'a rendu célèbre. En 1993, le propriétaire suédois de la marque cédait la commercialisation de son produit à Seagram, à la surprise du milieu publicitaire new-yorkais. A la même époque, Carillon acquérait Stolichnaya, la vodka russe par excellence. Un changement brutal qui prit des allures de défi pour Michel Roux. Tout le monde se demanda s'il pourrait s'éprendre de la marque qui n'était autre que la principale rivale d'Absolut. Pas de problème: sa carrière de jongleur n'allait pas s'arrêter en si bon chemin. Michel Roux s'attela aussitôt à la tâche avec l'énergie qui le caractérise. A l'heure actuelle, la vodka russe est sur le point de récupérer les parts de marché qu'elle avait perdues au profit de son concurrent suédois.

VV: On m'a dit que vous êtes né en France dans les Charentes, non loin de Cognac.

MR: Dans cette région de France, aucun endroit n'est vraiment éloigné des autres.

VV: Les Français aiment bien boire, surtout dans cette région. Votre but est-il de donner aux consommateurs américains le goût qu'ont vos compatriotes pour les vins fins et les spiritueux?

MR: Non, en aucun cas, la différence est bien trop grande. Les gens de ma région peuvent savourer un verre de vin pendant 10 à 20 minutes. Alors que les Français sirotent, les Américains avalent le contenu de leur verre d'un trait pour ressentir au plus vite l'effet de l'alcool.

VV: Avant Carillon, vous étiez gérant de boîtes de nuit et de restaurants au Texas. Cela a dû être un véritable choc culturel pour vous au début?

MR: C'est à ce moment-là que j'ai réalisé que la bouteille est tout aussi importante que le liquide qu'elle contient. Si les Français n'attachent que peu d'importance à la bouteille, les Américains sont très sensibles à l'aspect visuel.

VV: Mais il faut aussi tenir compte du facteur psychologique, émotionnel et socioculturel lié à une bouteille, et plus précisément à la marque. C'est là, je pense, que réside votre véritable force.

MR: En effet. La marque est quelque chose qui interpelle tous les sens. Toutefois, il faut savoir que lorsqu'un packaging est séduisant, les gens sont plus enclins à en apprécier le contenu.

VV: Qu'est-ce qui rend un emballage séduisant?

MR: Il doit fasciner, de l'étiquette à la forme de la bouteille en passant par la couleur de la boisson.

Lorsque nous avons retravaillé la bouteille bleue du gin Bombay, les spécialistes du marketing trouvaient que le verre teinté donnait au gin l'aspect d'une eau dentifrice. D'une eau dentifrice? Peut-être d'un parfum, mais certainement pas d'une eau dentifrice. D'ailleurs, bon nombre de parfumeurs s'inspirent des bouteilles de liqueur pour leurs flacons et vice versa.

VV: C'est vrai. Le flacon «cK One» de Calvin Klein, le «Thommy» d'Hilfiger et l'«America» d'Ellis rappellent les bouteilles de rhum ou de vodka. Sans oublier «Champagne», bien sûr, d'Yves Saint Laurent. Il y a peut-être une raison à cela. J'ai lu quelque part que l'eau de Cologne se composait autrefois d'un mélange de grappa et d'huiles essentielles. Elle pouvait donc être consommée comme une liqueur ou servir de parfum!

MR: Chez moi, en Provence, j'ai fabriqué de la vodka aromatisée à la lavande de mon jardin. Elle sent si bon qu'on s'en enduirait le corps! De plus, elle est aussi bonne qu'elle sent. A propos, saviez-vous qu'Andy Warhol se parfumait à l'Absolut? Il en a véritablement fait son parfum. Je ne sais pas s'il aimait son odeur ou s'il ne voulait pas dépenser d'argent pour un vrai parfum. Mais ne le mentionnez pas dans votre interview, certains lecteurs pourraient penser que nous les encourageons à se parfumer au gin et à boire du parfum!

VV: Pensez-vous commercialiser votre propre marque de vodka à la lavande?

MR: Je ne crois pas. J'ai suffisamment de travail avec les marques de Carillon. Le marketing, c'est comme le jardinage: si vous plantez trop de légumes au même endroit, ils manquent de place et ne donnent rien de bon. Il faut des années pour développer une marque. Parfois, il vaut mieux ne pas toucher à la bouteille ou à l'emballage. Changer un produit qui est entré dans la tradition requiert la plus grande prudence. Dans le cas du Grand Marnier par exemple, nous avons légèrement modernisé l'étiquette sans toutefois toucher à la bouteille qui symbolise à elle seule la qualité du produit.

VV: Comment faites-vous au juste? Comment procédez-vous pour introduire un produit typiquement suédois ou français dans la culture américaine?

MR: Le plus difficile consiste à expliquer aux propriétaires d'une marque comment leur produit est perçu dans un autre pays. Il était par exemple quasiment impossible d'expliquer aux responsables de Stolichnaya pourquoi il fallait ajouter de la vodka aromatisée à leur ligne de produits. Ils ont fait un blocage émotionnel et crié au sacrilège. Mon client français réagirait de même si je lui déclarais que nous mettons son Château de Beaulieu au réfrigérateur pour le servir frais.

VV: Votre tâche consiste donc à voyager à travers le monde pour exposer le style de vie américain?

MR: Tout à fait! C'est exactement ce que je fais. Il s'agit d'une croisade sans merci. Le succès d'une marque dépend de la façon dont j'explique à ses responsables comment leur produit est perçu aux Etats-Unis. Parfois, je m'en tire avec peu d'explications, dans d'autres cas, je dois faire plusieurs visites.

VV: Vous voyagez beaucoup?

MR: Je vais en France et en Angleterre six à sept fois par an et presque chaque mois en Russie.

VV: Comment se déroule la recherche?

MR: Ma recherche consiste à rester dans l'action, à suivre l'évolution du marché sur le terrain. Ma méthode n'a rien de très sophistiqué, mais elle marche. Pour créer une marque, il faut connaître la psychologie des consommateurs. Je discute par exemple avec les barmans et je bois des verres avec eux. Dans les sociétés de spiritueux français, les représentants suivent une cure de désintoxication au moins une fois par an. Leur métier exige qu'ils boivent avec les barmans et leurs clients. Il n'est donc pas rare qu'ils ingurgitent une quinzaine de verres sans s'en rendre compte. Aux Etats-Unis par contre, il est plus facile de nouer des contacts: vous pouvez en effet jouer rusé en vidant discrètement votre verre dans le premier pot de fleurs artificielles.

VV: Recourez-vous également aux stratégies classiques, avec leurs groupes cible et les sondages?

MR: Oui. A mon avis, elles ne servent à rien, mais nous y recourons tout de même.

VV: Quel est, selon vous, le profil du consommateur type de Stolichnaya?

MR: J'en distingue deux: le consommateur classique et celui qui préfère la version aromatisée. Le premier a 35 ans et plus, et le second est plus jeune, entre 21 et 40 ans. La Stolichnaya classique s'adresse aux hommes, l'aromatisée aux femmes. Bien entendu, tout cela est purement théorique. Je pense que, dans la vie, les choses suivent naturellement leur cours. Nous n'avons que très peu d'emprise sur les tendances. Autrefois, les jeunes regardaient ce que buvaient leurs aînés. Aujourd'hui, c'est l'inverse, les plus vieux imitent la relève. En outre, plus personne ne se sent vieux à 50 ou à 60 ans. Il est donc difficile de viser un public cible. De quel droit vais-je décourager un homme de commander une boisson destinée aux femmes? A mon avis, les différences s'estompent, les générations se fondent de plus en plus: les jeunes, les plus vieux, les hommes, les femmes.

VV: A quoi reconnaît-on un bon spécialiste du marketing?

MR: A l'instinct. Je n'ai jamais suivi de cours de marketing, mais je sais ce que veut le consommateur moyen, ce qu'il lui faut pour se détendre ou pour son confort. J'arrive à évaluer le potentiel d'un produit. D'ailleurs, Dieu soit loué, la publicité pour les boissons alcoolisées n'a pas forcément toujours quelque chose à voir avec le fait de boire. Dans le cas de la vodka Absolut, par exemple, nous avons joué la carte du divertissement et de l'effet mode, parce que cela répondait aux attentes du public.

VV: Quelles sont vos réactions, aujourd'hui, face à la campagne Absolut?

MR: Je n'étais pas responsable de la bouteille, mais uniquement de l'image qu'elle véhiculait. De plus, je n'étais pas seul, nous étions plusieurs à travailler sur ce projet. La plupart de mes collaborateurs de l'époque tentent d'ailleurs de tirer profit du succès de cette campagne, ce qui m'est bien égal.

VV: Aujourd'hui, Stolichnaya représente l'une de vos principales marques. Quels sont vos projets à cet égard?

MR: La bouteille Stolichnaya n'a rien d'exceptionnel. Enlevez l'étiquette, et il ne reste pas grand-chose. Elle rappelle n'importe quelle vodka russe. Ce qui n'est d'ailleurs pas forcément un mal. Dans la région de Cognac par exemple, cet élixir de premier choix n'est plus présenté dans des bouteilles stylisées, mais simples. Là-bas, simplicité rime avec qualité. La bouteille de Stolichnaya n'a rien d'exceptionnel non plus. Son étiquette, par contre, sort du lot et confère un attrait particulier au contenu. Par ailleurs, la campagne publicitaire «Freedom of vodka», avec ses peintures de l'avant-garde russe, renforce son caractère unique et authentique.

VV: Une marque peut-elle se développer sans publicité?

MR: Elle se met à plafonner à partir d'un certain moment. Le rôle de la publicité consiste à donner aux consommateurs un sentiment de bien-être. Toutefois, une marque a également besoin du bouche à oreille. Développer une marque signifie suivre un processus d'éducation interminable, travailler inlassablement d'un bar à l'autre, jour après jour.

VV: Vous parlez aux barmans, qui parlent à leur tour aux clients?

MR: Je ne me contente pas de parler aux barmans, je me mêle également à la clientèle. Il faut être suffisamment épris d'une marque pour la boire jour après jour.

VV: Etes-vous le moteur publicitaire de votre marque?

MR: On pourrait l'exprimer ainsi. Bien que, ces derniers temps, j'essaie de freiner un peu.

VV: Où trouvez-vous l'énergie nécessaire pour sortir tous les soirs?

MR: C'est un peu comme faire l'amour à 70 ans! Ma motivation réside dans la passion que j'éprouve à l'égard de mes marques et que j'essaie de faire partager à tout le monde. Dans notre entreprise, chaque employé devient l'ambassadeur de nos produits. C'est aussi simple que cela. Il y a quelques années, alors que je travaillais sur la campagne Absolut, je suis passé boire un verre chez des amis. A peine arrivé, ils m'ont servi de la Stolichnaya. J'ai tourné les talons aussi sec! Je ne pouvais pas supporter qu'ils boivent la marque concurrente. Promouvoir une marque, c'est aussi la vivre. Je ne sais pas pourquoi certaines personnes n'arrivent pas à le comprendre.

VV: Développer une marque, c'est un peu comme faire du jardinage?

MR: Oui, pour moi, c'est pareil. Je viens de la campagne, je suis un homme de la terre. Tous les matins, je contrôle l'état de mes salades, de mes fraises et de mes pommes de terre. Je vérifie la croissance de mes marques comme un paysan vérifie l'état de ses champs. Si vous voulez faire pousser quelque chose, il faut veiller au grain chaque jour. Une marque n'est pas un objet inanimé, elle demande beaucoup de soins et d'attention. A ce propos, j'aime beaucoup cette citation de Lamartine: «Objets inanimés, avez-vous donc une âme / Qui s'attache à notre âme et la force d'aimer?». Vous savez, ce métier n'a rien à voir avec le fait de boire de l'alcool, ce qui compte, c'est de croire en quelque chose et de vivre pour ça.

P.-D.G. DE CARILLON IMPORTERS, **MICHEL ROUX** A LARGEMENT CONTRIBUÉ AU DÉVELOPPEMENT, À LA DISTRIBUTION ET AU SUCCÈS DE NOMBREUX PRODUITS EUROPÉENS AUX ETATS-UNIS, DONT NOTAMMENT LES VODKAS STOLICHNAYA ET ABSOLUT, LE GRAND MARNIER, LES GIN BOMBAY ET BOMBAY SAPPHIRE ET PERLE DE BRILLET. GÉNIE DU MARKETING, ROUX EST ÉGALEMENT APPRÉCIÉ POUR SES QUALITÉS DE PHILANTHROPE, SA CONTRIBUTION AUX ARTS ET SON ENGAGEMENT CIVIQUE. SES ACTIVITÉS TANT SOCIALES QUE COMMERCIALES LUI ONT DÉJÀ VALU DE NOMBREUSES DISTINCTIONS.

VÉRONIQUE VIENNE VIT ET TRAVAILLE À BROOKLYN, NEW YORK, EN TANT QUE JOURNALISTE. NÉE À PARIS, ELLE Y ÉTUDIE L'ARCHITECTURE À L'ECOLE DES BEAUX-ARTS. APRÈS AVOIR TRAVAILLÉ PLUSIEURS ANNÉES À LA CONCEPTION D'EXPOSITIONS COMME DESIGNER, ELLE DEVIENT DIRECTRICE ARTISTIQUE DES MAGAZINES *INTERIORS*, *PARENTING* ET *SELF*. ELLE ÉCRIT DES ARTICLES CONSACRÉS AU DESIGN ET AUX TENDANCES CULTURELLES POUR DIVERSES PUBLICATIONS.

PAGE 2 ART DIRECTOR: *Barrie Tucker* DESIGNERS: *Jody Tucker, Barrie Tucker* AGENCY: *Tucker Design* CLIENT: *Negociants New Zealand* PRODUCT PHOTOGRAPHER: *Steve Keough* ILLUSTRATOR: *Maire Smith* DESIGN/PRODUCTION YEAR: *1994* BRANDS CARRIED: *Nautilus, Twin Islands* ■ *The agency needed to create a brand identity and packaging for a range of quality New Zealand wines for international sales. To create a striking presentation, the agency created a dynamic main label with the edges forming waves together with the shell icon as a separate label.* • *Die Aufgabe bestand in der Schaffung einer Markenidentität und Verpackung einer Reihe von neuseeländischen Qualitätsweinen für den internationalen Markt. Die Lösung: zwei Etiketten, von denen das eine wellenförmige Ränder hat, während das andere eine Muschel darstellt.* ▲ *Identité visuelle et packaging créés pour des vins néo-zélandais de qualité destinés à l'exportation. L'agence créa également deux étiquettes, l'une aux bords ondulés, l'autre en forme de coquillage.*

PAGE 4 ART DIRECTOR/DESIGNER: *Edi Berk* AGENCY: *Krog* PRODUCT PHOTOGRAPHER: *Janet Puksic* CLIENT: *Kratochwill* PRINTER: *Pgt Vecko* DESIGN/PRODUCTION YEAR: *1992* BRANDS CARRIED: *Svetlo, Pivo, Kratochwill* ■ *The agency wanted to create a classic beer label which would look like it had been created 100 years ago.* • *Hier ging es um die Gestaltung eines klassischen Bieretiketts im Stil von vor 100 Jahren.* ▲ *L'objectif était de créer une étiquette de bière classique au look rétro.*

PAGE 6 ART DIRECTOR/DESIGNER: *Roger Akroyd* AGENCY: *Michael Peters Limited* CLIENT: *Courvoisier S.A.* ■ *Understated graphics enhance the elegance of this unique bottle structure. The product is a new brand designed to compete with other cognac products in the Chinese and Taiwanese markets.* • *Zurückhaltende Graphik unterstreicht hier die Eleganz der Flasche. Es geht um eine neue Cognac-Marke, die es mit der Konkurrenz auf dem chinesischen und dem taiwanesischen Markt aufnehmen muss.* ▲ *Nouvelle marque de cognac lancée sur les marchés chinois et taïwanais. Le graphisme discret souligne l'élégance de la bouteille.*

PAGE 14 ART DIRECTOR: *Steve Sandstrom* DESIGNERS: *Steve Sandstrom, George Vogt* AGENCY: *Wieden & Kennedy* CLIENT: *McKenzie River Corporation/Black Star Beer* ■ *Historical packaging for a new beer to be used in an advertising campaign about the beer's fabulous (but fictitious) past. The designers had to work backwards from the present packaging. The bottles are antiques with new "antiqued" labels applied.* • *Ein neues Bier in historisch anmutender Verpackung, die in einer Werbekampagne über die fabelhafte (aber erfundene) Tradition des Bieres verwendet werden sollte. Die Gestalter mussten für einmal nicht modernisieren, sondern sich rückwärts orientieren. Die Flaschen sind alt, das Etikett wurde auf antik getrimmt.* ▲ *Packaging d'une nouvelle bière, également destiné à une publicité qui devait en retracer le passé fabuleux (mais fictif). La tâche des créatifs ne consista pas à moderniser l'image du produit, mais à faire revivre la tradition en utilisant des bouteilles anciennes et en créant une étiquette au charme suranné.*

PAGES 20-23 ART DIRECTOR: *Bill Cahan* DESIGNERS: *Kevin Roberson, Sharrie Brooks* AGENCY: *Cahan & Associates* CLIENT: *Boisset USA* TYPEFACE: *Univers, Officina, Din Neuzeit Grotesk, Handlettering* DESIGN/PRODUCTION YEAR:

1996 BRANDS CARRIED: *Alcatraz Ale & Lager* ■ *The packaging conveys the character of the Prohibition era, as many inmates of Alcatraz Penitentiary were arrested for bootlegging alcohol. It was designed to look as if it had been produced by the prisoners themselves. The bottle's metallic coating and regimental typography distinguishes it from other beers.* • *Thema ist die Zeit der Prohibition, als viele Schwarzbrenner im berüchtigten Alcatraz-Gefängnis landeten. Die Verpackung sieht aus, als hätten die Insassen sie selbst gestaltet. Der metallische Überzug und die spezielle Typographie sorgen dafür, dass sich das Bier eindeutig von der Konkurrenz unterscheidet.* ▲ *Le design rappelle l'époque de la prohibition, durant laquelle de nombreux distillateurs clandestins se retrouvèrent derrière les barreaux de la célèbre prison d'Alcatraz. L'habillage métallisé de la bouteille et la typographie démarquent cette bière des produits concurrents.*

PAGE 24 ART DIRECTOR: *Mark Chittenden* DESIGNER: *Elaine Barbook* AGENCY: *Design In Action* CLIENT: *Scottish Courage* ■ *A new premium, lager-based product targeting women.* • *Ein neues, belles Bier, dessen Verpackung vor allem Frauen ansprechen soll.* ▲ *Packaging d'une nouvelle bière blonde qui s'adresse principalement aux femmes.*

PAGE 25 ART DIRECTOR: *Bill Chiaravalle* DESIGNERS: *Stefanie Choi, Jeff Welsch, James Tee, Melissa Taylor* AGENCY: *Landor Associates* ILLUSTRATOR: *Larry Duke* CLIENT: *Bert Grant's* PRINTER: *Source Packaging, Hammer Lithograph*

PAGE 26 ART DIRECTOR/DESIGNER: *Jack Gernsheimer* AGENCY: *Partners Design, Inc.* PRODUCT PHOTOGRAPHER: *Peter Olson* CLIENT: *Neversink Brewery* TYPEFACE: *Copperplate* DESIGN YEAR: *1996*

PAGE 27 ART DIRECTOR: *Mary Lewis* AGENCY: *Lewis Moberly* CLIENT: *Bass* DESIGN YEAR: *1995* ■ *This ale, similar to a stout, was designed to compete with brands such as Guinness Draught Bitter and Boddingtons.* • *Dieses Ale, das einem Malzbier ähnelt, sollte sich gegen zwei populäre Konkurrenzprodukte in Grossbritannien durchsetzen.* ▲ *Ce packaging devait permettre à une ale de se démarquer de ses deux principales concurrentes sur le marché des bières brunes fortes en Grande-Bretagne.*

PAGES 28-29 ART DIRECTOR/DESIGNER: *Dan Olson* AGENCY: *Duffy Design* PRODUCT PHOTOGRAPHER: *Leo Tushaus* CLIENT: *Flagstone Brewery* ■ *The assignment was to brand, package and promote a southeastern regional specialty beer that would capture the imagination of a predominantly male, urban, and somewhat upscale microbrew consumer. References to bravery, glory, and honor reflect the brand's historically based personality.* • *Hier ging es um den gesamten Auftritt des Produktes einer Kleinbrauerei, die vor allem die vorwiegend männlichen, städtischen Biertrinker der Region ansprechen wollte. Mut, Ruhm und Ehre sind Themen, die dem Produkt einen historischen Charakter verleihen.* ▲ *L'agence avait pour tâche de créer l'identité visuelle d'une spécialité régionale, qui s'adresse principalement à des hommes aisés vivant en milieu urbain. Bravoure, gloire et honneur confèrent un caractère historique à cette bière.*

PAGE 30 (LEFT) ART DIRECTOR: *Joe Duffy* DESIGNER: *Kobe* AGENCY: *Duffy Design* CLIENT: *The Stroh Brewery* DESIGN

YEAR: *1994* ■ *The client wanted to introduce a pale malt beverage with a higher alcohol content. Anvil is marketed to 21-34-year-old blue-collar male consumers who need a compelling reason to try a new brand. It was designed to be not too trendy or ethnically oriented to ensure longer product life.* ● *Packungsgestaltung für die Einführung eines hellen Malzbiers mit höheren Alkoholgehalt. Zielgruppe sind 21- bis 34jährige Arbeiter, die einen guten Grund brauchen, um eine neue Marke zu probieren. Das Design durfte weder zu modisch noch ethnisch orientiert sein, um über längere Zeit aktuell zu bleiben.* ▲ *Design réalisé pour le lancement d'une ale à forte teneur en alcool. Cette bière blonde s'adresse à des ouvriers âgés de 21 à 34 ans, généralement fidèles à leur marque de bière. Pour assurer une longue durée de vie au produit, le design ne devait pas être trop moderne et présenter un caractère universel.*

PAGE 30 (RIGHT) ART DIRECTOR: *Joe Duffy* DESIGNER: *Missy Wilson* AGENCY: *Duffy Design* ILLUSTRATOR: *Michael Schwab* CLIENT: *The Stroh Brewery* ■ *The client wanted to introduce a malt liquor for a younger and hipper segment of the ice beer market. The agency used bright colors and bold type and imagery to set itself apart from other brands.* ● *Mit leuchtenden Farben und kraftvoller Typographie soll diese Verpackung für ein neues Produkt vor allem junge Konsumenten von «Eisbier» ansprechen.* ▲ *L'agence a utilisé des couleurs vives et une typographie marquante pour cette nouvelle bière maltée destinée aux jeunes amateurs d'«ice beer».*

PAGE 31 ART DIRECTOR: *Neil Powell* DESIGNERS: *Neil Powell, Alan Leusink* AGENCY: *Duffy Design* ILLUSTRATOR: *Neil Powell* CLIENT: *The Stroh Brewery* DESIGN YEAR: *1994* ■ *The objective was to create a package design which would convey to the consumer that this brand is a premium, top-quality beer which is bottled in limited batches. The bottle design is somewhat characteristic of a "sample bottle" and the label is fashioned after a quality control form which is signed and stamped by the brewmaster.* ● *Durch diese Verpackung sollte dem Kunden vermittelt werden, dass es sich um ein preisgekröntes, erstklassiges Bier handelt, das in limitierten Mengen abgefüllt wird. Die Flasche erinnert an eine Musterflasche, und das Etikett sieht aus wie ein Qualitätskontrollformular, das vom Braumeister unterschrieben und abgestempelt wurde.* ▲ *Objectif de l'agence: conférer un caractère prestigieux à cette bière haut de gamme produite en petite quantité. La bouteille rappelle un échantillon, et son étiquette ressemble à un formulaire de contrôle-qualité signé et estampillé par le maître-brasseur.*

PAGE 32 ART DIRECTOR: *Joe Duffy* DESIGNER: *Alan Leusink* AGENCY: *Duffy Design* ILLUSTRATOR: *Alan Leusink* CLIENT: *Molson Brewery* ■ *This design for a bold and agressive beverage was targeted to an urban Canadian audience.* ● *Diese Verpackung für ein kräftiges Bier sollte städtische Konsumenten in Kanada ansprechen.* ▲ *Design conçu pour une bière forte commercialisée au Canada.*

PAGE 33 ART DIRECTOR: *Joe Duffy* DESIGNERS: *Alan Leusink, Kobe* AGENCY: *Duffy Design* ILLUSTRATOR: *Kobe* CLIENT: *The Stroh Brewery* DESIGN YEAR: *1994* ■ *Design for a new microbrew.* ● *Flaschengestaltung für eine neue Biermarke einer Kleinbrauerei.* ▲ *Design pour une nouvelle marque de bière fabriquée par une microbrasserie.*

PAGE 34 CREATIVE DIRECTOR/ART DIRECTOR: *Jose A. Serrano* DESIGNERS: *Jose A. Serrano, Miguel Perez* AGENCY: *Mires Design* ILLUSTRATOR: *Tracy Sabin* CLIENT: *Bordeaux Printers* ■ *Bordeaux wine bottle labels promotion.* ● *Werbung mit Etiketten für Bordeaux-Weine.* ▲ *Etiquettes réalisées pour la promotion de vins de Bordeaux.*

PAGE 35 ART DIRECTORS/DESIGNERS: *Thomas Fairclough, Tom Antista, John Marota* AGENCY: *Antista Fairclough Design* PRODUCT PHOTOGRAPHER: *Michael West* CLIENT: *Anheuser-Busch, Inc.* BRANDS CARRIED: *Rio Cristal* ■ *Design for a beer produced for South America. The design is rich and festive in detail and beer cues, which supports the beer as a premium brew with superior taste.* ● *Flaschengestaltung für ein Bier, das für den südamerikanischen Markt bestimmt ist. Das üppige, festlich ausgeschmückte Etikett verspricht ein erstklassiges Bier von hervorragendem Geschmack.* ▲ *Bouteille créée pour une bière destinée au marché sud-américain. L'étiquette raffinée évoque un esprit de fête et positionne cette bière comme une boisson de qualité supérieure.*

PAGE 36 ART DIRECTORS: *Shirley Chapman, Leon Jones* DESIGNER: *Ed Johnson* AGENCY: *Chapman & Jones* PRODUCT PHOTOGRAPHER: *Jeffrey Michaels* ILLUSTRATOR: *Shirley Chapman* CLIENT/MANUFACTURER: *Yosemite Brewing Company* PRINTER: *Group #1 (label)* TYPEFACE: *Astaire Plain, Palatino Roman* DESIGN YEAR: *1995* PRODUCTION YEAR: *1996* BRANDS CARRIED: *Yosemite Beer* ■ *The design needed to reflect the majestic beauty of Yosemite National Park. Yosemite Falls, Bridal Veil Falls and El Capitan had to be in the illustration. The snow in the mountains and the green terrain convey an ice cold, natural, robust taste. The tall, lean typeface echoes the tall, towering pines. The "YB" within the label enables the client to use the icon for specialty advertising items.* ● *Das Thema der Illustration ist die Schönheit des Yosemite National Parks in der Sierra Nevada, Kalifornien. Die Yosemite- und Bridal-Veil-Wasserfälle und El Capitan sollten unbedingt auf dem Etikett sein. Die grüne Landschaft und die schneebedeckten Berge suggerieren ein kühles, natürliches, kräftiges Bier. Hohe, schmale Buchstaben erinnern an die grossen, mächtigen Kiefern. Das «YB»-Zeichen im Etikett eignet sich gut für diverses Werbematerial.* ▲ *Thème de l'illustration: la beauté majestueuse du Yosemite National Park situé dans la sierra Nevada, Californie. Les chutes d'eau de Yosemite et de Bridal Veil ainsi que El Capitan devaient absolument figurer sur l'étiquette. Le paysage verdoyant et les montagnes enneigées confèrent un caractère frais, puissant et naturel à cette bière. Les initiales «YB» intégrées à l'étiquette peuvent également être réutilisées sur divers supports publicitaires.*

PAGE 37 (TOP) ART DIRECTORS/DESIGNERS: *Thomas Fairclough, Tom Antista, John Marota* AGENCY: *Antista Fairclough Design* PRODUCT PHOTOGRAPHER: *Michael West* CLIENT: *Anheuser-Busch, Inc.* DESIGN/PRODUCTION YEAR: *1996* BRANDS CARRIED: *Winter Brew* ■ *The design for this holiday brew had to suggest a microbrewery look with imagery that captures an outdoor, snowy Christmas scene. The high detail of the label suggests the handcrafted quality of an old-time classic.* ● *Flaschenausstattung für ein Bier, das von einer Kleinbrauerei für die Weihnachtszeit lanciert wurde. Die verschneite Landschaft und sorgfältige Ausführung* des Etiketts sorgen für die gewünschte Stimmung und den Eindruck einer Qualität aus der guten alten Zeit. ▲ Bière fabriquée par une microbrasserie pour les fêtes de fin d'année. Le paysage enneigé et le soin apporté à l'étiquette confèrent une touche traditionnelle au produit.

PAGE 37 (MIDDLE) ART DIRECTORS: *John Marota, Thomas Fairclough, Tom Antista* DESIGNER: *Thomas Fairclough* AGENCY: *Antista Fairclough Design* PRODUCT PHOTOGRAPHER: *Michael West Photography* CLIENT: *Anheuser-Busch, Inc.* ■ The packaging was developed from 1800s resource material from the Anheuser-Busch archives. This brand was developed to compete with microbreweries. ● Die Verpackung wurde auf der Basis von Material aus den Archiven von Anheuser-Busch aus der Zeit um 1800 entwickelt. Die Marke muss sich im Markt der Biere von Kleinbrauereien durchsetzen. ▲ L'agence s'est inspirée des archives de Anheuser-Busch datant de 1800 pour créer ce design. Cette marque de bière a été développée pour concurrencer les microbrasseries.

PAGE 37 (BOTTOM) ART DIRECTORS: *John Marota, Thomas Fairclough* DESIGNER: *Thomas Fairclough* AGENCY: *Antista Fairclough Design* PRODUCT PHOTOGRAPHER: *Michael West Photography* CLIENT: *Anheuser-Busch, Inc.* ■ This packaging design uses festive colors and shapes to convey the holiday spirit. ● Eine speziell für die Weihnachtsfeiertage entworfene Verpackung. ▲ Packaging spécialement créé pour les fêtes de fin d'année.

PAGES 38, 39 ART DIRECTORS: *John Marota, Thomas Fairclough, Tom Antista* DESIGNER: *Thomas Fairclough* AGENCY: *Antista Fairclough Design* PRODUCT PHOTOGRAPHER: *Michael West Photography* ILLUSTRATOR: *Ezra Tucker* CLIENT: *Anheuser-Busch, Inc.* ■ The packaging was developed from 1800s resource material from the Anheuser-Busch archives. This brand was developed to compete with microbreweries. ● Die Verpackung wurde auf der Basis von Material aus den Archiven von Anheuser-Busch aus der Zeit um 1800 entwickelt. Die Marke muss sich im Markt der Biere von Kleinbrauereien durchsetzen. ▲ L'agence s'est inspirée des archives de Anheuser-Busch datant de 1800 pour créer ce design. Cette marque de bière a été développée pour concurrencer les microbrasseries.

PAGE 40 (TOP) ART DIRECTORS: *John Marota, Thomas Fairclough* DESIGNER: *Thomas Fairclough* AGENCY: *Antista Fairclough Design* PRODUCT PHOTOGRAPHER: *Michael West Photography* CLIENT: *Anheuser-Busch, Inc.* ■ The packaging was developed from 1800s resource material from the Anheuser-Busch archives. This brand was developed to compete with microbreweries. ● Die Verpackung wurde auf der Basis von Material aus den Archiven von Anheuser-Busch aus der Zeit um 1800 entwickelt. Die Marke sollte sich im Markt der Biere von Kleinbrauereien durchsetzen. ▲ L'agence s'est inspirée des archives de Anheuser-Busch datant de 1800 pour créer ce design. Cette marque de bière a été développée pour concurrencer les microbrasseries.

PAGE 40 (MIDDLE) ART DIRECTORS: *Jerry Andelin (Hal Riney & Partners), Primo Angeli* DESIGNER: *Mark Jones* AGENCY: *Primo Angeli Inc.* PRODUCT PHOTOGRAPHER: *June Fouché* ILLUSTRATOR: *Bruce Wolfe* CLIENT: *Hal Riney & Partners* DESIGN YEAR: *1995* TYPOGRAPHER: *Mark Jones*

PAGE 40 (BOTTOM) ART DIRECTORS: *John Marota, Thomas Fairclough* DESIGNER: *Thomas Fairclough* AGENCY:

Antista Fairclough Design PRODUCT PHOTOGRAPHER: *Michael West Photography* CLIENT: *Anheuser-Busch Inc.* ■ Elephant Red was developed to compete with red lager beers. Power and high alcohol content were conveyed through the graphic presentation. ● Die graphische Präsentation für dieses spezielle amerikanische Bier reflektiert den kräftigen Geschmack und den hohen Alkoholgehalt. ▲ Le graphisme de cette bière américaine reflète le goût puissant de la Red Beer et sa forte teneur en alcool.

PAGE 41 ART DIRECTORS: *Jerry Andelin (Hal Riney & Partners), Primo Angeli* DESIGNER: *Mark Jones* AGENCY: *Primo Angeli Inc.* PRODUCT PHOTOGRAPHER: *June Fouché* ILLUSTRATOR: *Bruce Wolfe* CLIENT: *Hal Riney & Partners* DESIGN YEAR: *1995* TYPOGRAPHER: *Mark Jones*

PAGE 42 ART DIRECTOR/DESIGNER: *Andrew Cawrse* AGENCY: *Cawrse & Effect* CLIENT: *Self-promotion*

PAGE 43 (TOP) ART DIRECTOR: *David Curtis* DESIGNERS: *David Curtis, Rick Jansen* AGENCY: *Curtis Design* CLIENT: *Miller Brewing Company*

PAGE 43 (MIDDLE) ART DIRECTORS: *Peter Di Donato, Don Childs* AGENCY: *Di Donato Associates* ILLUSTRATOR: *Rich Lo* CLIENT: *Goose Island Beer Company* PRINTER: *Inland Label/Zumbiel Carton* TYPEFACE: *Trajan, Copperplate, Kunstler Script, Modern No. 20* ■ Created for the retail launch of the product, this packaging is intended to communicate craft-brewed quality, to establish memorable shelf presence, and to create a system for product line expansion. ● Hier ging es um die Einführung einer Marke. Die Flaschenausstattung sollte die hohe Braukunst seiner Hersteller verdeutlichen und sich zudem für eine Erweiterung der Produktlinie eignen. ▲ Créée à l'occasion du lancement de la marque dans les commerces de détail, cette bouteille devait souligner le savoir-faire du fabricant et se prêter à l'extension de la gamme.

PAGE 43 (BOTTOM) ART DIRECTOR: *Michael Osborne* DESIGNER: *Christopher Lehmann* AGENCY: *Michael Osborne Design* PRODUCT PHOTOGRAPHER: *Tony Stromberg* ILLUSTRATOR: *Christopher Lehmann* CLIENT: *St. Stan's Brewing Co.* PRINTER: *Crown Packaging, Louis Roesch Co.* TYPEFACE: *Stymie, Copperplate* ■ Packaging created for the client's newest product and brand extension. ● Packungsgestaltung für ein neues Produkt innerhalb einer Linie. ▲ Design réalisé dans le cadre de l'extension de la marque.

PAGE 44 ART DIRECTOR: *Mary Lewis* DESIGNER: *David Beard* AGENCY: *Lewis Moberly* CLIENT: *Bass Plc.* ■ The packaging for this premium lager made with champagne yeast aims to reflect its difference from other beers. The bottle features a punt, reflective of a champagne bottle, and a black foil collar. Graphics are screened directly onto etched dark green glass to reinforce the product's unique champagne character. ● Die Verpackung für dieses Bier, das mit Champagner-Hefe hergestellt wird, sollte den Unterschied zu anderen Bieren verdeutlichen. Die gesamte Flaschenausstattung unterstreicht den einzigartigen Champagner-Charakter des Produktes. ▲ Packaging d'une bière brassée avec de la levure de champagne. Créée dans l'esprit des bouteilles de champagne, la bouteille souligne le caractère spécifique du produit.

PAGE 45 ART DIRECTOR/DESIGNER: *Roger Akroyd* AGENCY: *Michael Peters Ltd.* CLIENT: *Sibra S.A.* ■ *Packaging for light beer targeting young consumers* ● *Mit dieser Verpackung für ein leichtes Bier sollen vor allem die jungen Konsumenten angesprochen werden.* ▲ *Le packaging de cette bière légère vise principalement un public cible jeune.*

PAGES 46, 47 ART DIRECTOR/DESIGNER: *Don Sibley* AGENCY: *Sibley/Peteet Design* PRODUCT PHOTOGRAPHER: *Dick Patrick* ILLUSTRATOR: *Tom Hough* CLIENT: *The Gambrinus Company* PRINTER: *Inland Printing* DESIGN/PRODUCTION YEAR: *1996* BRANDS CARRIED: *Shiner, Corona*

PAGE 48 ART DIRECTORS: *Debbie Douglas, Ian McIlroy* DESIGNER: *Graham Walker* AGENCY: *EH6 Design Consultants* CLIENT: *Tennent Caledonian Breweries*

PAGE 49 ART DIRECTOR: *Rain Pikand* DESIGNER: *Andrus Lember* AGENCY: *Division* PRODUCT PHOTOGRAPHER: *Jaak Kadak* ILLUSTRATOR: *Rain Pikand* CLIENT: *Saku Brewery, Ltd.* PRINTER: *Lauttasaaren Paino* TYPEFACE: *Handlettering, M Grotesk, Engravers Gothic* ■ *This packaging was created for an Estonian brewery which produces specialty beers for events, festivals, or seasons. Saku Porter was produced for the Christmas season.* ● *Packungsgestaltung für eine Brauerei aus Estland, die Spezialbiere für verschiedene Anlässe oder Jahreszeiten herstellt. Saku Porter ist ein Bier für die Weihnachtszeit.* ▲ *Bouteille créée pour une brasserie estonienne, qui fabrique des bières spéciales pour des festivals et autres manifestations ainsi qu'en fonction des saisons de l'année, telle la Saku Porter destinée aux fêtes de fin d'année.*

PAGE 50 ART DIRECTOR/DESIGNER: *Bruno Hohmann* AGENCY: *Coomes Dudek* PHOTOGRAPHER/ILLUSTRATOR: *Amy Blythe* CLIENT: *Stoney Creek*

PAGE 51 ART DIRECTOR: *Glenn Tutssel* DESIGNER: *Garrick Hamm* AGENCY: *Tutssels* CLIENT: *Inch's Cider Ltd.* BRANDS CARRIED: *White Lightning, Stonehouse* ■ *Building on the growth of the cider market, this design was created to reflect traditional handmade values. A rough, painted label was used to achieve this effect.* ● *Angesichts des wachsenden Marktes für Apfelwein ging es hier um die Betonung sorgfältiger Handarbeit, was durch das gemalte Etikett erreicht wurde.* ▲ *Sur le marché du cidre en pleine expansion, le packaging devait mettre en avant les qualités d'un produit fabriqué dans le respect de la tradition. L'étiquette peinte de manière artisanale crée l'effet recherché.*

PAGE 52 AGENCY: *Cato Design Inc.* PRODUCT PHOTOGRAPHER: *Mark Rayner* CLIENT: *Foster's* DESIGN/PRODUCTION YEAR: *1996* ■ *The agency needed to create a design that would give the brand a bold new identity.* ● *Die Aufgabe bestand in der Schaffung eines neuen, starken Images für die Biermarke.* ▲ *L'agence avait pour tâche de créer une nouvelle identité pour cette marque de bière.*

PAGE 53 (LEFT) ART DIRECTOR: *Mark Wickens* DESIGNER: *Simon Coker* AGENCY: *Wickens Tutt Southgate* ILLUSTRATOR: *Anton Morris* CLIENT: *Allied Breweries* ■ *The strategy was to create a design for a high-strength lager which would reflect how targeted consumers see themselves–as connoisseurs of lager. The design was based on craftsmens' hallmarks, giving the brand a more refined positioning in its market.* ● *Die Strategie für dieses rela-*

tiv starke blonde Bier bestand in einem Design, das genau das Bild reflektieren sollte, das die Lieberhaber dieses Biers von sich haben: das eines Connoisseurs. Thema der Gestaltung ist daher das Brauhandwerk, wodurch das Bier als anspruchsvolles Qualitätsprodukt positioniert wird. ▲ *Pour promouvoir cette bière blonde relativement forte, la stratégie consista à créer un design qui reflète l'image que ses amateurs ont d'eux-mêmes, à savoir celle de connaisseurs. L'accent a été mis sur la tradition et le savoir-faire des maîtres-brasseurs pour positionner cette bière comme un produit de qualité supérieure.*

PAGE 53 (RIGHT) AGENCY: *Cato Design Inc.* PRODUCT PHOTOGRAPHER: *Mark Rayner* CLIENT: *Foster's* DESIGN/PRODUCTION YEAR: *1996* ■ *The agency needed to create a design that would give the brand a bold new identity.* ● *Die Aufgabe bestand in der Schaffung eines neuen, starken Images für die Biermarke.* ▲ *L'agence avait pour tâche de créer une nouvelle identité pour cette marque de bière.*

PAGE 54 ART DIRECTOR/DESIGNER: *Brody Hartman* AGENCY: *Sterling Group* PRODUCT PHOTOGRAPHER: *Ron Ruo* CLIENT: *Miller Brewing Co.* ■ *Packaging for a beer made without additives or preservatives.* ● *Packungsgestaltung für ein Bier, das ohne Zusätze oder Konservierungsmittel hergestellt wird.* ▲ *Packaging d'une bière fabriquée sans additif ni conservateur.*

PAGE 55 AGENCY: *Cato Design Inc.* PRODUCT PHOTOGRAPHER: *Mark Rayner* CLIENT: *Cascade Brewery* ■ *This design utilizes the tiger (the tasmanian devil), a famous tasmanian icon.* ● *Das hier eingesetzte Tiger-Motiv (der tasmanische Teufel) ist eine berühmte tasmanische Ikone.* ▲ *Illustration d'un tigre, célèbre emblème tasmanien symbolisant le diable.*

PAGE 56 (TOP) CREATIVE DIRECTOR: *Primo Angeli* ART DIRECTORS: *Carlo Pagoda, Primo Angeli* DESIGNERS: *Carlo Pagoda, Primo Angeli, Doug Hardenburgh* AGENCY: *Primo Angeli Inc.* CLIENT: *Matilda Bay Brewing Company* DESIGN YEAR: *1989* ■ *The agency needed to build a brand identity that would be seen as traditional, established, masculine, and special but not trendy. The solution was to use a unique label shape in two colors, printed directly on the bottle. Simple, strong typography was used to support and reinforce the beer's image.* ● *Gewünscht war ein Markenauftritt, der traditionell, etabliert, maskulin und aussergewöhnlich, aber keinesfalls modisch wirken sollte. Die Lösung bestand in einem einzigartigem Etikett, das in zwei Farben direkt auf die Flasche gedruckt wurde. Einfache, ausdrucksvolle Typographie unterstützt das angestrebte Image des Biers.* ▲ *Le client désirait une identité de marque qui ait un caractère traditionnel, masculin et original, mais en aucun cas moderne. La solution consista à utiliser une seule étiquette bicolore, directement imprimée sur la bouteille. La typographie, simple et puissante, renforce l'image de cette bière.*

PAGE 56 (BOTTOM) AGENCY: *Cato Design Inc.* PRODUCT PHOTOGRAPHER: *Mark Rayner* CLIENT: *DB Breweries Limited*

PAGE 57 ART DIRECTOR/DESIGNER: *Ken Cato* AGENCY: *Cato Design Inc.* ILLUSTRATORS: *Lena Gan, Neil Moorhouse* CLIENT: *South Pacific Brewery* ■ *Can and bottle design for an imported beer. The illustration was meant to* evoke the area of origin. ● Ausstattung für die Dose und Flasche eines Importbiers. Die Illustration ist ein Hinweis auf das Ursprungsland. ▲ Canette et bouteille d'une bière d'importation. L'illustration évoque le pays d'origine.

PAGE 58 ART DIRECTORS: *David Wombell, Bernard Gormley* DESIGNER: *Paul Davies* AGENCY: *Ziggurat* CLIENT: *Asda Stores Plc.* ■ *Bottles for a pilsener sold by British stores. The illustration refers to the industrial city of Dortmund.* ● *Flaschengestaltung für ein Pils, das von einer Ladenkette in Grossbritannien angeboten wird. Die Illustration zeigt die Stadt Dortmund.* ▲ *Bouteilles d'une bière de Pilsen commercialisée en Grande-Bretagne. L'illustration représente la ville de Dortmund.*

PAGE 59 ART DIRECTOR: *Thomas Sakol* DESIGNER: *Anita Bassie* AGENCY: *Group M* CLIENT: *Dock Street Brewing Company* TYPEFACE: *Bodoni* ■ *The goal was to make the product stand out from those of other microbreweries and to reposition the beer among premium European beers. The three primary colors represent the three varieties of beer produced by the client.* ● *Aufgabe war es, dem Produkt einer Kleinbrauerei zum Image eines speziellen, erstklassigen europäischen Biers zu verhelfen. Die drei Grundfarben stehen für die drei Biersorten der Brauerei.* ▲ *L'objectif était de positionner cette bière fabriquée par une microbrasserie comme l'une des meilleures d'Europe. Les trois couleurs primaires symbolisent les trois sortes de bières proposées.*

PAGE 60 ART DIRECTORS: *Woody Pirtle, John Klotia* DESIGNERS: *Seung Il Choi, Sha-Mayne Chan* AGENCY: *Pentagram Design* PRODUCT PHOTOGRAPHER: *Richard Bachmann* ILLUSTRATOR: *Woody Pirtle* CLIENT: *Flying Fish Brewing Co.* DESIGN YEAR: *1995* PRODUCTION YEAR: *1996* BRANDS CARRIED: *Flying Fish Extra Pale Ale* ■ *The objective was to not look like every other microbrewery. Instead of backward-looking imagery–sheaves of barley, revolutionary war heroes–the client wanted something unabashedly modern. The whimsical label signals a different, edgier product.* ● *Um sein Bier von den Konkurrenzprodukten anderer Kleinbrauereien zu unterscheiden, wollte der Kunde statt der üblichen Gerstengarben oder Heldenbilder einen radikal modernen Auftritt. Das verrückte Etikett signalisiert ein Produkt mit eigenem Profil.* ▲ *Pour démarquer sa bière des produits concurrents, le client souhaitait un concept résolument moderne en lieu et place des images classiques illustrant des gerbes d'orge ou des héros virils. L'originalité de l'étiquette est à l'image du produit.*

PAGE 61 ART DIRECTOR: *Woody Pirtle* DESIGNER: *Seung Il Choi* AGENCY: *Pentagram Design* PRODUCT PHOTOGRAPHER: *Richard Bachmann* ILLUSTRATOR: *Woody Pirtle* CLIENT: *Flying Fish Brewing Co.* DESIGN YEAR: *1995* PRODUCTION YEAR: *1996* BRANDS CARRIED: *Flying Fish Extra Pale Ale*

PAGE 62 ART DIRECTOR/DESIGNER: *Steve Davies* AGENCY: *Davies Hall* ILLUSTRATOR: *Steve Davies* CLIENT: *Sainsbury's* ■ *The agency was briefed to create a strong and credible brand identity for a supermarket's French ale. The agency developed a cockerel motif which is reminiscent of poster-style French graphics and reinforces the provenance of the ale. Earthy, traditional colors were used to reflect the beer's flavor.* ● *Gewünscht war ein starker, glaubwürdiger Auftritt für ein französisches Ale, das von einem Supermarkt angeboten wird. Die Lösung be-*

stand in dem Hahnmotif als Symbol für das Ursprungsland, während erdige, traditionelle Farben eine Vorstellung vom Geschmack des Biers vermitteln sollen. ▲ *L'agence avait pour mission de créer une image forte et crédible pour une ale de supermarché française. L'emblème du coq fut retenu pour symboliser l'origine du produit tandis que les tons chauds évoquent la saveur de la bière.*

PAGE 63 ART DIRECTOR: *Glenn Tutssel* DESIGNER: *Garrick Hamm* AGENCY: *Tutssels* CLIENT: *Bass Brewers* TYPEFACE: *Gill, Universe* ■ *The silver labels and ice skating lines of this design reflect the product identity of this new "ice beer."* ● *Die silbrigen Etiketten und die Schlittschuhspuren der Flaschengestaltung reflektieren die Eigenschaften dieses neuen «Eis-Biers».* ▲ *Les étiquettes argentées et les traces de patins à glace évoquent les qualités de cette nouvelle «ice beer».*

PAGE 64 ART DIRECTOR/DESIGNER: *John Mark* AGENCY: *Creativstudio Mark & Neuosad* ILLUSTRATOR: *Willi Mitschke* CLIENT: *Privatbrauerei Fritz Egger*

PAGE 65 ART DIRECTOR/DESIGNER: *Miguel Angel Pellot* AGENCY: *EJE Sociedad Publicitaria* PRODUCT PHOTOGRAPHER: *Ernesto Robles* CLIENT: *Bacardi Martini*

PAGE 66 ART DIRECTOR/DESIGNER: *David Hughes* AGENCY: *Poppe Tyson* PRODUCT PHOTOGRAPHER: *Tom Gigliotti* CLIENT: *Penn Brewery* PRINTER: *General Press* DESIGN/PRODUCTION YEAR: *1996* ■ *This new fest bier was created in honor of and to celebrate St Nikolaus.* ● *Ein neues Festbier zu Ehren des heiligen St. Nikolaus.* ▲ *Nouvelle bière de fête créée en l'honneur de Saint-Nicolas.*

PAGE 67 ART DIRECTOR/DESIGNER: *David Hughes* AGENCY: *Poppe Tyson* PRODUCT PHOTOGRAPHER: *Tom Gigliotti* CLIENT: *Penn Brewery* PRINTER: *General Press* DESIGN/PRODUCTION YEAR: *1995* ■ *This design was meant to suggest German folklore.* ● *Deutsche Folklore war das Thema dieser Flaschenausstattung.* ▲ *Packaging décliné sur le thème du folklore allemand.*

PAGE 68 ART DIRECTOR: *Kip Reynolds* DESIGNER: *Tom Sutherland* AGENCY: *Landor Associates, London* CLIENT: *Del Haize* ■ *Bottle design for a Belgian beer. The bottle in the foreground displays a label which has been reworked; the bottle in the background shows a new design. The agency wanted to keep the light, silver equity from the previous label while adding a masculine feel and historical reference.* ● *Flaschengestaltung für ein belgisches Bier. Beim Etikett der Flasche im Vordergrund handelt es sich um eine Überarbeitung des Designs; die Flasche im Hintergrund wurde neu gestaltet.* ▲ *Bouteille d'une bière belge. La bouteille au premier plan présente l'étiquette, reliftée; celle à l'arrière-plan, le nouveau design.*

PAGE 69 (TOP) ART DIRECTOR/DESIGNER: *Jack Hermsen* AGENCY: *Hermsen Design Associates* ILLUSTRATOR: *Raymond Jaundrau* CLIENT: *Rubinoff Importing Co.* PRINTER: *Package Master Limited* MANUFACTURER: *Glacier Brewing Co.* ■ *Design for a Canadian beer.* ● *Ausstattung für ein kanadisches Bier.* ▲ *Concept réalisé pour une bière canadienne.*

PAGE 69 (BOTTOM) ART DIRECTOR/DESIGNER: *Mary Lewis* AGENCY: *Lewis Moberly Design Consultants* CLIENT: *Tesco*

■ *Bottle design and carrier carton for beer from Ireland's oldest brewery. The agency used black-and-white illustrations and an old-fashioned form to lend a nostalgic touch.* ● *Gestaltung der Flasche und des Tragkartons für ein Bier der ältesten Brauerei Irlands. Die Schwarzweiss Illustrationen und die altmodische Form sorgen für den gewünschten nostalgischen Touch.* ▲ *Bouteille et carton réalisés pour une bière fabriquée par la plus ancienne brasserie irlandaise. Les illustrations en noir et blanc et la forme vieillotte confèrent une touche nostalgique.*

PAGE 70 (TOP) ART DIRECTOR/DESIGNER: *Barrie Tucker* AGENCY: *Tucker Design* PRODUCT PHOTOGRAPHER: *Steve Keough* ILLUSTRATORS: *Barrie Tucker, Elizabeth Schlooz* CLIENT: *The South Australian Brewing Co.* PRINTER: *Collotype Labels* DESIGN/PRODUCTION YEAR: *1992* BRANDS CARRIED: *Southwark, West End, Eagle* ■ *The agency needed to create a quality presentation for the premium product of an old South Australian brand. To achieve the desired perception of quality, the agency used deep green, rich red and gold colors with the green bottle.* ● *Aufgabe war die Schaffung eines anspruchsvollen Auftritts für ein erstklassiges Bier aus südaustralischer Produktion. Die gewünschte Wirkung wird hier durch die Kombination der satten Farben mit der grünen Flasche erzielt.* ▲ *Le client, une marque australienne réputée, souhaitait une présentation soignée pour son produit haut de gamme. L'effet recherché est obtenu par la combinaison des couleurs – vert foncé, rouge profond et or.*

PAGE 70 (BOTTOM) ART DIRECTOR/DESIGNER: *Jeffrey Caldewey* AGENCY: *Caldewey Design* CLIENT: *Strapramen Brewery* DESIGN YEAR: *1991* PRODUCTION YEAR: *1996*

PAGE 71 ART DIRECTOR: *Glenn Tutssel* DESIGNER: *Garrick Hamm* AGENCY: *Tutssels* ILLUSTRATOR: *Colin Frewin* CLIENT: *Tennent Caledonian Breweries*

PAGE 72 ART DIRECTOR/DESIGNER: *Fred Tieken* AGENCY: *Tieken Design and Creative Services* PRODUCT PHOTOGRAPHER: *Paul Markow* ILLUSTRATOR: *Tad A. Smith* CLIENT: *Black Mountain Brewing Company* ■ *The design is meant to suggest an afternoon in a Mexican cantina. The lime green background suggests the traditional lime wedge taken with Mexican beer.* ● *Das Design dieser Flasche soll an einen Nachmittag in einer mexikanischen* Cantina *erinnern. Der limonengrüne Hintergrund ist eine Anspielung auf den Brauch, mit dem mexikanischen Bier einen Limonenschnitz zu servieren.* ▲ *La bouteille devait évoquer une chaude après-midi dans une* cantina *mexicaine. La couleur du fond rappelle la tranche de citron vert que les Mexicains ajoutent à la bière.*

PAGE 73 ART DIRECTORS/DESIGNERS: *Thomas Fairclough, Tom Antista, John Marota* AGENCY: *Antista Fairclough Design* PRODUCT PHOTOGRAPHER: *Michael West* ILLUSTRATOR: *Kevin Newman* CLIENT: *Anheuser-Busch, Inc.* BRANDS CARRIED: *Roscoe's Red* ■ *This label was developed to compete with European microbrew imports exploding on the US market. The beer was positioned as a spirited English ale, featuring unexpected detail and signature traits of authentic English beer pubs. The "Roscoe" figure represents a streetwise, tough yet charming character.* ● *Die Marke wurde als Antwort auf die Importschwemme von Bier europäischer Kleinbrauereien auf dem US-Markt*

lanciert. Positioniert wurde das Bier als temperamentvolles britisches Ale, was durch das schlichte, glaubwürdige, in Details jedoch überraschende Design mit Anspielungen auf authentische englische Bier-Pubs unterstützt wird. Die «Roscoe»-Figur steht für den mit allen Wassern gewaschenen, aber sympathischen Grossstadttyp.* ▲ *Etiquette créée pour démarquer le produit des nombreuses bières d'importation européennes qui ont envahi le marché américain. Pour positionner cette bière anglaise comme une ale unique en son genre, l'agence a choisi un design simple évoquant les pubs anglais. Le personnage de Roscoe représente un homme à la peau dure mais sympathique.*

PAGE 74 ART DIRECTOR: *Gail Sharp* DESIGNER: *Tony Blurton* AGENCY: *Michael Peters Limited* ILLUSTRATORS: *Anthony Sidwell, Frances Barrett, Colin Frewin* CLIENT: *Fine Fare*

PAGE 75 ART DIRECTOR: *Kai Funck* AGENCY: *Funck Kommunikationsdesign* PRODUCT PHOTOGRAPHER: *Kai Funck* CLIENT: *Holsten* ■ *Packaging incorporating bottle, glass, and can in one product.* ● *Flasche, Glas und Dose in einem Produkt vereint.* ▲ *Bouteille, verre et canette réunis en un seul produit.*

PAGES 76, 77 ART DIRECTORS: *Yutaka Sasaki, Kahei Kiyono* DESIGNER: *Toru Kubo* AGENCY: *Nippon Design Center* CLIENT: *Asahi Breweries, Ltd.*

PAGE 78 ART DIRECTOR: *Jack Anderson* DESIGNERS: *Jack Anderson, Larry Anderson, Bruce Branson-Meyer* AGENCY: *Hornall Anderson Design Works, Inc.* PRODUCT PHOTOGRAPHER: *Tom McMackin* ILLUSTRATOR: *Mark Summers* CLIENT: *Rhino Chasers* PRINTER: *Zumbiel; Inland Printing* MANUFACTURER: *General Paper Products* DESIGN/PRODUCTION YEAR: *1996* ■ *The client needed a beer label that conveyed a free-spirited, "extremist" yet handcrafted quality that projected a "go for it," "no fear" attitude. A bold medallion was designed with the image of a rhino head charging out from the curl of a wave. "Rhino" is the slang term from the 1950s for surfers who would challenge extreme conditions.* ● *Gewünscht war ein Etikett, das Attribute wie unabhängig, extrem, überzeugt und furchtlos ausdrücken und dabei auf die sorgfältig gebraute Qualität hinweisen sollte. Das Medaillon mit dem aus einer Welle emportauchenden Kopf eines Nashorns symbolisiert die wilden Surfer der 50er Jahre, die extreme Bedingungen bevorzugten.* ▲ *L'étiquette devait évoquer la qualité du produit et des valeurs comme l'indépendance, la bravoure et le goût du risque. Le médaillon représentant la tête d'un rhinocéros émergeant au-dessus d'une vague symbolise les surfers des années 50 en mal de sensations fortes.*

PAGE 79 ART DIRECTOR: *James Sundstad* DESIGNERS: *Dan Saimo, James Sundstad* AGENCY: *Werkhaus Design* PRODUCT PHOTOGRAPHER: *Jim Linna* ILLUSTRATOR: *James Sundstad* CLIENT: *Emerald City Brewing Co.* DESIGN/PRODUCTION YEAR: *1993* BRANDS CARRIED: *Emerald City Ale, Post Alley Pale Ale* ■ *This design was created for a microbrew brand that would be perceived as uniquely "Seattle." The agency wanted to create a graphic language that blends traditional style with contemporary illustration.* ● *Diese Marke einer Kleinbrauerei sollte als typisch «Seattle» empfunden werden. Die graphische Lösung bestand in einer Mischung von traditionellem Stil und zeitgenössischer Illustration.* ▲ *Packaging d'une bière* américaine «typiquement Seattle». La solution graphique consista à marier style traditionnel et illustration contemporaine.

PAGE 80 ART DIRECTOR: *Mark Wickens* DESIGNER: *Simon Coker* AGENCY: *Wickens Tutt Southgate* PRODUCT PHOTOGRAPHER: *David Gill* ILLUSTRATORS: *Anton Morris (label), Peter Horridge (lettering)* CLIENT: *Black Sheep Brewery Plc* TYPEFACE: *Mixed-mainly handdrawn* DESIGN/PRODUCTION YEAR: *1993*

PAGE 81 ART DIRECTOR/DESIGNER: *Jack Hermsen* AGENCY: *Hermsen Design Associates* ILLUSTRATOR: *Bart Forbes* CLIENT: *Rubinoff Importing Co., Inc.* PRINTER: *Manville* MANUFACTURER: *Cerveceria Cuauhtemoc* ■ *The client wanted a strong, masculine image that would stimulate consumer interest. Keying off of the name, the illustration conveys a romantic southwestern image epitomized by the "vaquero." The logo was handlettered in a style reminiscent of intricately tooled leather.* ● *Hier ging es um ein starkes, maskulines Image, mit dem das Interesse des Konsumenten geweckt werden sollte. Die Illustration, eine Anspielung auf den Namen, zeigt ein romantisches Bild des Südwestens, verkörpert durch den vaquero". Der Stil des Logos mit dem handgeschriebenen Namenszug erinnert an Ledermarken.* ▲ *Le client souhaitait une image forte et virile à même d'éveiller l'intérêt du client. L'illustration, une allusion au nom, montre une image romantique du Sud-ouest, symbolisée par le vaquero. Le logo manuscrit fait penser à du cuir repoussé.*

PAGE 82 ART DIRECTOR/DESIGNER: *Taku Satoh* AGENCY: *Taku Satoh Design Office Inc.* CLIENT: *Kirin Brewery Company, Limited*

PAGE 83 ART DIRECTOR/DESIGNER: *Gregg Boling* AGENCY: *Dye, Van Mol and Lawrence* ILLUSTRATOR: *Jim Hsebi* CLIENT: *Jack Daniels* PRINTER: *Lithographics* DESIGN YEAR: *1996* ■ *The agency needed to explain this new beer's point of difference from other craft beers. This sales kit was created to be used by the sales force to reinforce the fact that the beer is aged with oak chips from barrel wood from Jack Daniel's whiskey.* ● *Hier ging es darum, die Einzigartigkeit dieses neuen Biers zum Ausdruck zu bringen. Das Material sollte dem Aussendienst der Brauerei helfen, den Kunden zu vermitteln, dass das Bier mit Eichenholzspänen der Fässer von Jack Daniels Whiskey gereift wird.* ▲ *Matériel publicitaire créé pour souligner la spécificité d'une nouvelle bière vieillie avec des copeaux de chêne provenant des fûts utilisés pour le whisky Jack Daniel.*

PAGE 84 (TOP) DESIGNER: *Christopher Hadden* AGENCY: *Christopher Hadden Design* ILLUSTRATOR: *Marty Braun* CLIENT: *Shipyard Brewing Co.* DESIGN/PRODUCTION YEAR: *1994*

PAGE 84 (BOTTOM) DESIGNER: *Christopher Hadden* AGENCY: *Christopher Hadden Design* ILLUSTRATOR: *Bruce Hutchison* CLIENT: *Shipyard Brewing Co.* DESIGN/PRODUCTION YEAR: *1993*

PAGE 85 ART DIRECTOR: *Charles Finkel* DESIGNER: *Bruce Hale* AGENCY: *Bruce Hale Design* CLIENT: *August Schell Brewing Co.* ■ *The challenge was to give this beer a 90-year heritage. The solution was to handletter an authentic label with the naïveté of a turn-of-the-century commercial artist.* ● *Um die 90jährige Tradition des*

Biers hervorzuheben, wurde ein handbeschriftetes Etikett im Stil der liebenswert naiven Werbung um die Jahrhundertwende kreiert. ▲ *Pour souligner la tradition séculaire de cette bière, l'agence a opté pour une étiquette calligraphiée dans le style des publicités naïves typiques du début de siècle.*

PAGE 86 ART DIRECTOR: *David Curtis* DESIGNERS: *David Curtis, Matt Sullivan* AGENCY: *Curtis Design* CLIENT: *The Stroh Brewery* PRINTER: *Precision Printing*

PAGE 87 ART DIRECTOR: *Eberhard Rapp* DESIGNER: *Joerg Bauer* AGENCY: *Leonhardt + Kern* PHOTOGRAPHER: *Dirk Olaf Wexel* CLIENT: *Schwaben Bräu Rob. Leicht KG* ■ *Bottle and label design for a special beer marketed each year during the Christmas season.* ● *Flasche und Etikett für ein spezielles Bier für die Weihnachtszeit.* ▲ *Bouteille et étiquette créées pour une bière de Noël.*

PAGE 88 ART DIRECTOR: *Barrie Tucker* DESIGNERS: *Barrie Tucker, Elizabeth Schlooz, Luci Giannattilio* AGENCY: *Tucker Design* CLIENT: *Carlton & United Breweries* ■ *Special gift packaging, menu and place card designed for the 100th anniversary of Foster's beer.* ● *Spezielle Geschenkverpackung, Speisekarte und Platzkarte zum hundertjährigen Bestehen von Foster's Bier.* ▲ *Emballage cadeau, menu et cartons créés pour le centième anniversaire des bières Foster.*

PAGE 89 (TOP LEFT) ART DIRECTOR/DESIGNER: *Keith Harris* AGENCY: *Keith Harris Package Design* CLIENT: *Brauerei Frankenheim* PRINTER: *Töpfer Kulmbach GmbH* TYPEFACE: *Plantin Bold Cond.* ■ *This redesign of an established altbier brand also acknowledged the existing brand identity.* ● *Die Aufgabe der Agentur bestand in der Überarbeitung des Designs für ein etabliertes Altbier, ohne das alte Erscheinungsbild der Marke zu vernachlässigen.* ▲ *La tâche de l'agence consistait à revisiter le packaging de cette bière réputée sans trahir l'ancienne identité visuelle.*

PAGE 89 (TOP RIGHT) ART DIRECTORS/DESIGNERS: *Thomas Fairclough, Tom Antista, John Marota* AGENCY: *Antista Fairclough Design* PRODUCT PHOTOGRAPHER: *Michael West* CLIENT: *Anheuser-Busch, Inc.* ■ *The packaging was developed from 1800s resource material from the Anheuser-Busch archives. This brand was developed to compete with microbreweries.* ● *Die Verpackung wurde auf der Basis von Material aus den Archiven von Anheuser-Busch aus der Zeit um 1800 entwickelt. Die Marke muss sich im Markt der Biere von Kleinbrauereien durchsetzen.* ▲ *L'agence s'est inspirée des archives de Anheuser-Busch datant de 1800 pour créer ce design. Cette marque de bière a été développée pour concurrencer les microbrasseries.*

PAGE 89 (BOTTOM LEFT) ART DIRECTORS/DESIGNERS: *Thomas Fairclough, Tom Antista, John Marota* AGENCY: *Antista Fairclough Design* PRODUCT PHOTOGRAPHER: *Michael West* CLIENT: *Anheuser-Busch, Inc.* ■ *This packaging takes the traditional oval format and incorporates a wave; a two-tone texture in the background enhances the design.* ● *Für diese Verpackung wurde das traditionelle ovale Format des Auftraggebers übernommen.* ▲ *Packaging reprenant le format ovale, signe distinctif du client.*

PAGE 89 (BOTTOM RIGHT) ART DIRECTOR: *Mark Oliver* DESIGNERS: *Mark Oliver, Patty Devlin-Driskel* AGENCY: *Mark Oliver, Inc.* CLIENT: *Firestone Walker Brewing Co.*

PRINTER: *Lois Roesch* TYPEFACE: *Copperplate Gothic, Poppl* DESIGN YEAR: *1996* ■ *This bottle for a handcrafted brew was designed to convey a sense of American heritage.* ● *Bei dieser Flasche für ein von Hand gebrautes Bier sollte die amerikanische Herkunft betont werden.* ▲ *Packaging d'une bière brassée de façon artisanale. L'origine américaine du produit devait clairement ressortir.*

PAGES 90, 91 ART DIRECTOR: *Bill Caban* DESIGNER: *Kevin Roberson* AGENCY: *Caban & Associates* CLIENT: *Boisset USA* MANUFACTURER: *Crown Packaging* TYPEFACE: *Futura* DESIGN/PRODUCTION YEAR: *1996* BRANDS CARRIED: *Apollo Ale & Lager* ■ *The agency attempted to capture the spirit and importance of the historic Apollo mission. The blue bottle and simple graphics suggest the vastness of space. The packaging was positioned to reflect high quality from a sophisticated microbrewery, to counter the traditional branding trend.* ● *Hier wurde versucht, den Geist und die Bedeutung der Apollo-Mission zum Audruck zu bringen. Die blaue Flasche und die schlichte Graphik symbolisieren die Weite des Weltraums. Die Verpackung für eine anspruchsvolle Kleinbrauerei steht im Kontrast zu dem Trend, diesen Produkten ein traditionelles Image geben zu wollen.* ▲ *L'agence souhaitait rendre l'esprit et le caractère historique de la mission Apollo. La bouteille bleue et le graphisme simple symbolisent l'immensité de l'espace. Le packaging devait indiquer qu'il s'agit d'une bière de qualité supérieure et rompre avec l'image classique de ce type de produit.*

PAGE 92 ART DIRECTOR/DESIGNER: *David Lancashire* ILLUSTRATOR: *Godfrey Fawcett* CLIENT: *Berri Renmaro Wines* DESIGN/PRODUCTION YEAR: *1989*

PAGE 98 ART DIRECTOR/DESIGNER: *John Blackburn* AGENCY: *Blackburn's Limited* CLIENT: *Orchid Drinks*

PAGE 99 ART DIRECTOR: *Barrie Tucker* DESIGNERS: *Barrie Tucker, Jody Tucker* AGENCY: *Tucker Design* PRODUCT PHOTOGRAPHER: *Steve Keough* ILLUSTRATORS: *Jody Tucker, Barrie Tucker* CLIENT: *Orlando Wyndham* PRINTER/MANUFACTURER: *Pak Pacific* DESIGN/PRODUCTION YEAR: *1991* BRANDS CARRIED: *Orlando, Jacobs Creek, Gramps, Morris, Montrose, Richmond Grove* ■ *The agency needed to develop a new brand identity logotype for Morris of Rutherglen and to package the three fortified wines to relate the history of the five generations of the Morris family. The agency created packages which fit together as a small range while each pack tells with contemporary flair the story of the family's heritage.* ● *Die Aufgabe bestand in der Schaffung eines neuen Markenzeichens für Morris of Rutherglen, ein traditionsreiches Weingut, sowie in der Verpackung für drei mit Most vergärte Weine. Es entstand eine kleine Verpackungsfamilie, wobei jede einzelne Verpackung die Geschichte der fünf Generationen des Familienbetriebes erzählt.* ▲ *Création d'une nouvelle identité visuelle pour un producteur de vin réputé et d'une famille d'emballages pour trois vins vinés. Les packagings devaient illustrer de manière séduisante la longue tradition de la maison, cultivée depuis cinq générations.*

PAGE 100 ART DIRECTOR/DESIGNER: *Patti Britton* AGENCY: *Britton Design* PRODUCT PHOTOGRAPHER: *M. J. Wickham* CLIENT: *Viansa Winery* PRINTER: *Bolling & Finke* TYPEFACE: *Augustea Open* DESIGN/PRODUCTION YEAR: *1992* ■ *The agency wanted to accentuate the sculptural elongated*

shape of the bottle. A segmented label was created. The upper label consists of a fresco in a classical Renaissance inverted "U" form and the lower label was reserved for typography. ● *Hier ging es um die Betonung der besonderen Flaschenform. Das obere Etikett besteht aus einem Renaissance-Fresko, während das untere ypographisch gelöst ist.* ▲ *L'objectif était de mettre en valeur les formes sculpturales de la bouteille. Le bandeau illustre une fresque Renaissance, et l'étiquette se distingue par sa typographie soignée.*

PAGE 101 ART DIRECTOR/DESIGNER: *Patti Britton* AGENCY: *Britton Design* PRODUCT PHOTOGRAPHER: *Mitch Rice* ILLUSTRATOR: *Brion Ward* CLIENT: *Viansa Winery* PRINTER: *Paganini Enteprises* TYPEFACE: *Augustea Open* DESIGN/PRODUCTION YEAR: *1996* ■ *To accentuate the round, feminine bottle with two flanged rows at the bottom of the glass, an angled label featuring the goddess Athena was chosen. An illustration of a Mediterranean scene with Athena appears on the band of type.* ● *Um die runde, feminine Flasche mit den beiden Zierrändern zu betonen, entschied man sich für ein dreieckiges Etikett, das die Göttin Athena zeigt. Eine Illustration mit einer mediterranen Szenerie und Athena erscheinen auf dem beschrifteten unteren Etikett.* ▲ *Pour souligner les formes rondes et féminines de la bouteille, l'agence a choisi une étiquette triangulaire illustrant la déesse Athéna. Le bandeau illustre une scène méditerranéenne et Athéna.*

PAGE 102 ART DIRECTOR/DESIGNER: *Patti Britton* AGENCY: *Britton Design* PRODUCT PHOTOGRAPHER: *Mitch Rice* CLIENT: *Viansa Winery* PRINTER: *Northwestern Graphics* TYPEFACE: *Augustea Open* DESIGN/PRODUCTION YEAR: *1996* ■ *To complement the color of the glass, the agency used an orange label with a fresco from the 15th century positioned above a white band containing the typography.* ● *Als Ergänzung zur Farbe des Glases wurde ein orangefarbenes Etikett mit einem Fresko aus dem 15 Jahrhundert gewählt; darunter ein weisses Etikett mit Schrift.* ▲ *Pour faire ressortir la couleur du verre, l'agence a choisi une étiquette orange illustrant une fresque du XVe siècle tandis que la typographie se détache sur un fond blanc.*

PAGE 103 (TOP LEFT) ART DIRECTOR/DESIGNER: *Patti Britton* AGENCY: *Britton Design* ILLUSTRATOR: *Patti Britton* CLIENT: *Ferrari-Carano* PRINTER: *Bolling & Finke* TYPEFACE: *Janson Open* DESIGN/PRODUCTION YEAR: *1993* ■ *Since the wine is named after the rich orange/red Tuscan, Italy earth color, the die-cut label conveys "from the earth."* ● *Der Name des Weins und das Etikett beziehen sich auf die rote Erde der Toskana.* ▲ *Le nom du vin et l'étiquette gaufrée évoquent la terre rouge de la Toscane.*

PAGE 103 (TOP RIGHT) ART DIRECTOR/DESIGNER: *Patti Britton* AGENCY: *Britton Design* PRODUCT PHOTOGRAPHER: *Mitch Rice* CLIENT: *Viansa Winery* PRINTER: *Bolling & Finke* TYPEFACE: *Augustea Open, Centaur* DESIGN/PRODUCTION YEAR: *1995* ■ *The tall Italian flint bottle complements the wine's soft color. The label features an image of a 15th century fresco from the walls of Viansa.* ● *Die hohe italienische Flint-Flasche ergänzt den sanften Farbton des Weins. Auf dem Etikett ist ein Fresko aus dem 15. Jahrhundert aus Viansa zu sehen.* ▲ *Bouteille italienne en flint-glass mettant en valeur la robe du vin. L'étiquette illustre une fresque de Viansa datant du XVe siècle.*

PAGE 103 (BOTTOM LEFT) ART DIRECTOR/DESIGNER: *Patti Britton* AGENCY: *Britton Design* CLIENT: *Viansa Winery* PRINTER: *Bolling & Finke* TYPEFACE: *Augustea Open* DESIGN YEAR: *1991* PRODUCTION YEAR: *1992* ■ *Since this wine is a blend of Primitivo, Zinfandel, and Charbano, the union is symbolized by three Renaissance curved arches over a 15th century fresco. The Italian bottle chosen has an unusually large lip without the traditional foil capsule.* ● *Die drei Renaissance-Bögen über einem Fresko aus dem 15. Jahrhundert symbolisieren die drei Traubensorten (Primitivo, Zinfandel und Charbano), aus denen dieser Wein gekeltert wurde. Die ausgewählte italienische Flasche hat einen ungewöhnlich langen Hals ohne die übliche Metallkappe.* ▲ *Les trois arcs Renaissance coiffant une fresque du XVe siècle symbolisent les trois cépages entrant dans la composition de ce cru (primitivo, zinfandel et charbano). La bouteille italienne se distingue par son col allongé et l'absence de calotte plombée.*

PAGE 103 (BOTTOM RIGHT) ART DIRECTOR/DESIGNER: *Patti Britton* AGENCY: *Britton Design* PRODUCT PHOTOGRAPHER: *M. J. Wickham* CLIENT: *Viansa Winery* PRINTER: *Bolling & Finke* TYPEFACE: *Augustea Open* DESIGN YEAR: *1992* PRODUCTION YEAR: *1993* ■ *This Sangiovese wine, Piccolo Toscano, meaning "little Tuscan" features a tapered bottle with a bright red capsule. The label features a 15th century fresco within an ornamental oval.* ● *Diese sich nach oben verjüngende Flasche mit der leuchtend roten Kappe enthält Sangiovese-Wein aus der Toskana. Ein Fresko aus dem 15. Jahrhundert schmückt das Etikett.* ▲ *Bouteille effilée et bouchée avec une capsule rouge vif pour un vin de Toscane. L'étiquette illustre une fresque du XVe siècle.*

PAGES 104, 105 ART DIRECTOR/DESIGNER: *David Lancashire* AGENCY: *David Lancashire Design* ILLUSTRATOR: *David Lancashire* CLIENT: *Self-promotion* ■ *Self-promotional gift of wine produced by the design studio for friends, clients, and suppliers.* ● *Geschenkverpackung für einen Wein, den ein Designstudio an Freunde, Kunden und Lieferanten verschickte.* ▲ *Emballage-cadeau d'un vin envoyé par une agence de design à des amis, à des clients et à des fournisseurs.*

PAGE 106 ART DIRECTOR: *John Swieter* DESIGNERS: *Jim Vogel, John Swieter* AGENCY: *Swieter Design U.S.* ILLUSTRATOR: *Jim Vogel* CLIENT: *Hinkle Vineyards* ■ *The primary design objective was to design a label that reflected the culture and geographic characteristics of the vineyard. Based in New Mexico, this small handcrafted wine has a small and loyal following.* ● *Das Etikett für diesen Wein reflektiert die Kultur und die geographische Lage des Weingutes, das sich in Neumexiko befindet. Der in kleinen Mengen produzierte Wein hat eine kleine, sehr loyale Anhängerschaft.* ▲ *L'étiquette de ce vin évoque la situation géographique du vignoble au Nouveau-Mexique et ses caractéristiques. Produit en petite quantité, ce nectar compte un petit nombre d'amateurs fidèles.* ▲*mall handcrafted wine had a very small and loyal following.*

PAGE 107 ART DIRECTOR/DESIGNER: *Paul Haslip* AGENCY: *HM+E Incorporated* ILLUSTRATOR: *Gerard Gauci* CLIENT: *Grenville Printing* ■ *Wine bottle and carton sent by a printer to clients at Christmas. The label and carton demonstrate the craftsmanship of the printer, drawing a comparison with that of a vintner.* ● *Weinflasche und Karton, das Weihnachtsgeschenk eines Druckers für seine Kunden. Etikett und Karton demonstrieren das Können der Druckerei, das mit dem des Winzers verglichen wird.* ▲ *Bouteille de vin et carton envoyés aux clients d'une imprimerie comme cadeau de Noël. L'étiquette et le carton mettent l'accent sur le savoir-faire de l'imprimeur, le comparant à celui du vigneron.*

PAGE 108 (TOP) ART DIRECTOR: *Mary Lewis* DESIGNER/ ILLUSTRATOR: *Amanda Lawrence* AGENCY: *Lewis Moberly* CLIENT: *Asda Stores* ■ *Packaging for a house brand of Spanish red wine.* ● *Verpackung für einen spanischen Rotwein, die Hausmarke einer Ladenkette.* ▲ *Packaging d'un vin espagnol, la marque maison d'une chaîne de magasins.*

PAGE 108 (BOTTOM) ART DIRECTOR: *Barrie Tucker* DESIGNERS: *Barrie Tucker, Jody Tucker* AGENCY: *Tucker Design* ILLUSTRATOR: *Jody Tucker* CLIENT: *Padthaway Estate* ■ *Packaging for a small winery in South Australia.* ● *Flaschengestaltung für ein kleines Weingut in Südaustralien.* ▲ *Bouteille créée pour un petit domaine viticole d'Australie-Méridionale.*

PAGE 109 (TOP) ART DIRECTOR: *Piero Ventura* DESIGNER: *Rossella Rabuffi* AGENCY: *Immagine Design* CLIENT: *Antiche Fattorie Fiorentine* ■ *Wooden box as gift packaging and bottle livery for an Italian red wine.* ● *Holzschachtel als Geschenkverpackung und Flaschenausstattung für einen italienischen Rotwein.* ▲ *Boîte de bois utilisée comme emballage-cadeau et habillage d'une bouteille de vin rouge italien.*

PAGE 109 (BOTTOM) ART DIRECTOR: *Barrie Tucker* DESIGNERS: *Barrie Tucker, Elizabeth Schlooz* AGENCY: *Barrie Tucker Design* CLIENT: *David Wynn Wine Company* ■ *Labels created for a selection of Australian wines.* ● *Etiketten für eine Auswahl australischer Weine.* ▲ *Etiquettes créées pour une sélection de vins australiens.*

PAGE 110 ART DIRECTOR: *Glyn West* DESIGNER: *Lindsay Herbert* AGENCY: *Market + Design Ltd.* ILLUSTRATOR: *Lindsay Herbert* CLIENT: *Tesco Stores Ltd.* ■ *The directive was to produce package design (label and neck tag) for a premium range of sherries.* ● *Die Aufgabe bestand in der Schaffung der Verpackung (Etikett und Anhänger) für eine Familie erstklassiger Sherrys.* ▲ *Packaging créé pour une famille de sherries de qualité supérieure.*

PAGE 111 ART DIRECTOR/DESIGNER: *Mark Oliver* AGENCY: *Mark Oliver, Inc.* ILLUSTRATOR: *V. Courtland Johnson* CLIENT: *Firestone Vineyard* ■ *Packaging for a California red wine.* ● *Ausstattung für einen kalifornischen Rotwein.* ▲ *Packaging pour un vin rouge californien.*

PAGE 112 ART DIRECTOR/DESIGNER: *Jeffrey Caldewey* AGENCY: *Caldewey Design* CLIENT: *Goosecross Cellars* PRINTER: *Herdell Printing* TYPEFACE: *Custom*

PAGE 113 ART DIRECTOR/DESIGNER: *Michael Manwaring* AGENCY: *Michael Manwaring* CLIENT: *Hanna Winery* ■ *Packaging for a white wine.* ● *Flaschengestaltung für einen Weisswein.* ▲ *Packaging pour un vin blanc.*

PAGE 114 ART DIRECTOR: *Paola Dashwood* DESIGNER: *Derek Ventling* AGENCY: *Dashwood Design* PRODUCT PHOTOGRAPHER: *David Ogden* ILLUSTRATOR: *Gary Sullivan* CLIENT: *Montana Wines* PRINTER: *Panprint* TYPEFACE:

Boton, Zanzibar ■ *The packaging design was meant to be dynamic, contemporary, and bold in order to attract young wine drinkers.* ● *Gewünscht war eine dynamische, zeitgemässe und auffällige Verpackung, mit der vor allem junge Weintrinker angesprochen werden sollten.* ▲ *Packaging dynamique, moderne et accrocheur visant un public cible jeune.*

PAGE 115 ART DIRECTOR: *Michel Logoz* DESIGNER: *Jacques Zanoli* AGENCY: *Creation Communication* PRODUCT PHOTOGRAPHER: *Magali Koenig* ILLUSTRATOR: *Beat Brusch* CLIENT: *Provins Valais* ■ *Bottle design for wines from Valais, Switzerland.* ● *Flaschengestaltung für Weine aus dem Wallis, Schweiz.* ▲ *Bouteille créée pour des vins du Valais, Suisse.*

PAGE 116 DESIGNERS: *Jeffrey Caldewey, Dan MacLain, Jim Murphy* AGENCY: *Caldewey Design* ILLUSTRATOR: *Dan MacLain* CLIENT: *Fetzer Vineyards* PRINTER: *Bolling and Finke* TYPEFACE: *Handlettering, Copperplate* ■ *The torn, textured, handlettered label and proprietary bottle shape reflect the natural origin of this organically produced product.* ● *Das zerrissene, von Hand beschriftete Etikett und die eigenwillige Flaschenform reflektieren den natürlichen Ursprung dieses ökologisch produzierten Weines.* ▲ *L'étiquette manuscrite et déchirée ainsi que la forme particulière de la bouteille reflètent l'origine de ce vin de culture biologique.*

PAGE 117 DESIGNER: *Wayne Kosaka* AGENCY: *Kosaka Design* ILLUSTRATOR: *Nick Wilton* CLIENT: *Zaca Mesa Winery* PRINTER: *Blake Printery*

PAGE 118 ART DIRECTOR: *Keizo Matsui* DESIGNERS: *Keizo Matsui, Yuko Araki* AGENCY: *Keizo Matsui & Associates* CLIENT: *Yagi Shizou-Bu* PRINTER: *Kotobuki Seihan Co., Ltd.* ■ *This bottle and label design was created for a local Japanese sake company.* ● *Flasche und Etikett wurden für einen Sake entworfen, der für den japanischen Markt bestimmt ist.* ▲ *Bouteille et étiquette créées pour un saké commercialisé sur le marché japonais.*

PAGE 119 (TOP LEFT) ART DIRECTOR: *Akio Okumura* DESIGNER: *Mitsuo Ueno* AGENCY: *Packaging Create, Dentsu Inc.* CLIENT: *Gekkeikan* TYPEFACE: *Univers* ■ *This packaging was created for a Japanese sake.* ● *Packungsgestaltung für einen japanischen Sake.* ▲ *Packaging créé pour une marque de saké japonais.*

PAGE 119 (TOP RIGHT) ART DIRECTOR: *Akio Okumura* DESIGNER: *Emi Kajihara* AGENCY: *Packaging Create, Dentsu Inc.* CLIENT: *Gekkeikan* TYPEFACE: *Original* ■ *This packaging was created for Japanese sake.* ● *Packungsgestaltung für einen japanischen Sake.* ▲ *Packaging créé pour une marque de saké japonais.*

PAGE 119 (BOTTOM LEFT) ART DIRECTOR: *Keizo Matsui* DESIGNERS: *Keizo Matsui, Yuko Araki* AGENCY: *Keizo Matsui & Associates* CLIENT: *Yagi Shizou-Bu* PRINTER: *Kotobuki Seihan Co., Ltd.* ■ *This bottle and label design was created for a local Japanese sake company.* ● *Flaschenausstattung für einen Sake, der für den japanischen Markt bestimmt ist.* ▲ *Bouteille et étiquette créées pour un saké commercialisé sur le marché japonais.*

PAGE 119 (BOTTOM RIGHT) DESIGNER: *Toshio Kamitani* AGENCY: *TCD Corporation* PRODUCT PHOTOGRAPHER: *Toshio Kamitani* CLIENT: *Hakutsuru Sake Brewing Co., Ltd.*

TYPEFACE: *Mincyo* ■ *The packaging targets young women and is designed to reflect a sense of harmony with Japan's seasons.* ● *Diese Verpackung, die ein Gefühl mit Harmonie mit den Jahreszeiten in Japan vermitteln soll, richtet sich vor allem an junge Frauen.* ▲ *Ce packaging évoque l'harmonie avec les saisons au Japon et s'adresse aux jeunes femmes.*

PAGE 120 ART DIRECTOR: *Kristin Breslin Sommese* DESIGNER: *Rich Westover* AGENCY: *Art 376, Penn State University* PRODUCT PHOTOGRAPHERS: *Richard Ackley, Dwain Harbst* CLIENT: *Self-promotion* DESIGN/PRODUCTION YEAR: *1996* ■ *Self-promotion created to be given on Earth Day.* ● *Als Eigenwerbung verwendetes Geschenk zum Tag der Erde ("Earth Day") in den USA.* ▲ *Cadeau autopromotionnel créé à l'occasion de la journée de la Terre («Earth Day») aux Etats-Unis.*

PAGE 121 AGENCY: *Cato Design Inc.* PRODUCT PHOTOGRAPHER: *Mark Rayner* CLIENT: *Vinefera Services Pty Ltd* DESIGN/PRODUCTION YEAR: *1996* ■ *The agency chose to represent the wine with various game, giving a classy and distinguished image.* ● *Um dem Wein ein besonders Image zu geben, wählte man die Jagd bzw. Tiere zum Thema.* ▲ *Pour conférer une image distinguée au produit, l'agence a choisi la chasse comme thème central.*

PAGE 122 ART DIRECTOR/DESIGNER: *Tom Antista* AGENCY: *Antista Fairclough Design* PRODUCT PHOTOGRAPHER: *Jerry Burns* CLIENT: *Heinz Weber* DESIGN/PRODUCTION YEAR: *1992*

PAGE 123 ART DIRECTOR: *Kristin Breslin Sommese* DESIGNER: *Bryon Lomas* AGENCY: *Art 376, Penn State University* PRODUCT PHOTOGRAPHERS: *Richard Ackley, Dwain Harbst* CLIENT: *Self-promotion* DESIGN/PRODUCTION YEAR: *1996* ■ *Self-promotion created to be given away on Halloween.* ● *Geschenkverpackung aus Anlass des Halloween-Festes in den USA.* ▲ *Emballage-cadeau créé à l'occasion de la fête d'halloween aux Etats-Unis.*

PAGE 124 ART DIRECTORS/DESIGNERS: *Barrie Tucker, Jody Tucker* AGENCY: *Tucker Design* PRODUCT PHOTOGRAPHER: *Simon Vaughan* ILLUSTRATOR: *Jody Tucker (label)* CLIENT: *Southcorp Wines* PRINTER: *Five Star Press* DESIGN/PRODUCTION YEAR: *1995* BRANDS CARRIED: *Tulloch, Seppelt, Penfolds, Seaview, Rouge Homme, Wynns, Lindemans* ■ *Handmade design for a centenary dinner of a winery in the Hunter Valley.* ● *Von Hand gestaltetes Etikett für einen Wein, der zu einem speziellen Festessen gereicht wurde.* ▲ *Etiquette de vin réalisée de façon artisanale à l'occasion d'une grande réception.*

PAGE 125 ART DIRECTOR: *Kristin Breslin Sommese* DESIGNER: *Sandy DeMarco* AGENCY: *Art 376, Penn State University* PRODUCT PHOTOGRAPHERS: *Richard Ackley, Dwain Harbst* CLIENT: *Self-promotion* DESIGN/PRODUCTION YEAR: *1996* ■ *Self-promotion created to be given during the Christmas season.* ● *Als Weihnachtsgeschenk konzipierte Verpackung für einen Wein.* ▲ *Packaging autopromotionnel offert durant les fêtes de fin d'année.*

PAGE 126 ART DIRECTOR: *Barrie Tucker* DESIGNERS: *Barrie Tucker, Joe Marrapodi* AGENCY: *Tucker Design* PRODUCT PHOTOGRAPHER: *Steve Keough* CLIENT: *Saddler's Creek Winery* DESIGN YEAR: *1992* PRODUCTION YEAR: *1993* BRANDS CARRIED: *Bluegrass, Marrowbone, Watermark* ■ *Corporate identity and packaging for two dessert* *wines released for a restaurant and cellar door sales.* ● *Erscheinungsbild und Verpackung für zwei Weine, die für den Direktverkauf eines Restaurants bzw. eines Weinkellers bestimmt sind.* ▲ *Identité institutionnelle et packaging de deux vins destinés à la vente directe pratiquée dans un restaurant et sa cave.*

PAGE 127 ART DIRECTOR: *Barrie Tucker* DESIGNERS: *Barrie Tucker, Jody Tucker* AGENCY: *Tucker Design* PRODUCT PHOTOGRAPHER: *Steve Keough* ILLUSTRATORS: *Jody Tucker (label), Bob Bennett (finished art)* CLIENT: *Saddler's Creek Winery* DESIGN/PRODUCTION YEAR: *1994* BRANDS CARRIED: *Saddlers Creek, Bluegrass, Marrowbone, Watermark* ■ *Design presentation of red wine. To convey elegance, the agency used grass graphics superimposed on a handmade paper background.* ● *Das handgeschöpfte Papier und die Illustration des Etiketts für diesen australischen Rotwein sollen ein Gefühl von Eleganz vermitteln.* ▲ *Le papier de fabrication artisanale et l'illustration de l'étiquette confèrent un caractère élégant à ce vin rouge australien.*

PAGE 128 ART DIRECTOR: *Barrie Tucker* DESIGNERS: *Barrie Tucker, Jody Tucker* AGENCY: *Tucker Design* PRODUCT PHOTOGRAPHER: *Simon Vaughan* ILLUSTRATOR: *Barrie Tucker* CLIENT: *Samuel Smith & Son P/L* PRINTER: *Collotype Labels* DESIGN YEAR: *1994* PRODUCTION YEAR: *1996* BRANDS CARRIED: *Heggies, Pewsey Vale, Angas, Brut, Octavius, Oxford Landing, Antipodean* ■ *The agency needed to upgrade the existing package for a more sophisticated presentation. The illustration created in 1978 was torn from the old label and positioned on the bottle as an art print. The brand name and wine style were printed on the capsule.* ● *Hier ging es um die Überarbeitung einer Verpackung, der es an Eleganz mangelte. Die Illustration aus dem Jahre 1978 wurde aus dem alten Etikett gerissen und wie ein Kunstdruck auf der Flasche angebracht. Markenname und Weinsorte sind auf die Kappe gedruckt.* ▲ *L'agence avait pour tâche de rendre le packaging existant plus sophistiqué. L'illustration datant de 1978 a été arrachée de l'ancienne étiquette et apposée sur la bouteille comme une impression artistique. Le nom et le cépage figurent sur la capsule.*

PAGE 129 ART DIRECTOR: *Barrie Tucker* DESIGNER: *Hans Kohla* AGENCY: *Tucker Design* PRODUCT PHOTOGRAPHER: *Simon Vaughan* ILLUSTRATOR: *Hans Kohla* CLIENT: *Southcorp Wines* DESIGN YEAR: *1994* PRODUCTION YEAR: *1995* BRANDS CARRIED: *Seppelt, Penfolds, Rouge Homme, Wynns, Lindemans, Seaview, Tulloch* ■ *The client wanted to develop a brand name and striking packaging for a newly developed, young fortified wine to enter the market. The agency developed the concept of 375ml clear bottles to show the colors of the wines and design presentation to appeal to young buyers.* ● *Die Aufgabe bestand in der Entwicklung eines Markennamens und einer attraktiven Verpackung für einen neu entwickelten, jungen, mit Most versetzten Wein, der auf dem Markt eingeführt werden sollte. Die Lösung bestand in 375ml-Flaschen aus klarem, weissen Glas und einem Design, das vor allem junge Leute ansprechen sollte.* ▲ *La tâche de l'agence consista à développer un nom de marque et un packaging séduisant pour le lancement d'un vin viné sur le marché. Le design et les bouteilles de verre transparent d'une contenance de 375 ml visent un public cible jeune.*

PAGE 130 ART DIRECTOR: *Barrie Tucker* DESIGNERS: *Barrie Tucker, Jody Tucker* AGENCY: *Tucker Design* PRODUCT PHOTOGRAPHER: *Steve Keough* TYPOGRAPHER: *Joe Marrapodi* CALLIGRAPHER: *Claire Rose* CLIENT: *Samuel Smith & Son P/L* DESIGN/PRODUCTION YEAR: *1992* BRANDS CARRIED: *Yalumba, Heggies, Pewsey, Vale, Angas, Brut, Octavius, Oxford Landing* ■ *Brand identity and package presentation for a limited edition red wine named Octavius. A Roman numeral "I" was created for the first Octavius. The handwritten copy, embossed vintage and torn base of the labels suggests an exclusive, classic wine.* ● *Markenidentität und Packungsgestaltung für eine Sonderabfüllung roten Weins, Octavius genannt. Die römische «I» wurde für den ersten Octavius entworfen. Die dank der Handschrift, Prägungen und Beschädigungen antik wirkenden Etiketten sprechen von einem exklusiven, klassischen Wein.* ▲ *Identité de marque et packaging d'un vin rouge, l'Octavius, produit en petite quantité. Le «I» romain a été spécialement créé pour le premier Octavius. Les indications manuscrites, le gaufrage et le bord déchiré de l'étiquette évoquent un vin classique et prestigieux.*

PAGE 131 ART DIRECTOR/DESIGNER: *Barrie Tucker* AGENCY: *Tucker Design* PRODUCT PHOTOGRAPHER: *Simon Vaughan* ILLUSTRATOR: *Hans Kohla* CLIENT: *Southcorp Wines* PRINTER: *Collotype Labels* DESIGN YEAR: *1994* PRODUCTION YEAR: *1995* BRANDS CARRIED: *Seppelt, Penfolds, Seaview, Rouge Homme, Wynns, Lindemans, Tulloch* ■ *The client's Muscat and Tokay were prize-winning, but didn't sell with their old packaging. The agency utilized small 375ml bottles and a contemporary presentation. Stock sold out within weeks.* ● *Die Muskat- und Tokaierweine des Kunden hatten Prädikate erhalten, aber sie verkauften sich in der alten Verpackung nicht. Die Lösung bestand in kleinen 375ml-Flaschen mit einer zeitgemässen Ausstattung. Innerhalb von wenigen Wochen waren sämtliche Bestände ausverkauft.* ▲ *Bien que le muscat et le tokay du client aient été primés lors de concours, les ventes n'ont pas suivi en raison du packaging. Pour remédier à cette situation, l'agence a opté pour une présentation moderne et des bouteilles de 375 ml. En l'espace de quelques semaines, le stock était épuisé.*

PAGE 132 ART DIRECTOR/DESIGNER: *Barrie Tucker* AGENCY: *Tucker Design* PRODUCT PHOTOGRAPHER: *Simon Vaughan* ILLUSTRATOR: *Barrie Tucker* CLIENT: *Southcorp Wines* PRINTER: *Impresstik* DESIGN YEAR: *1994* PRODUCTION YEAR: *1995* BRANDS CARRIED: *Seppelt, Penfolds, Seaview, Wynns, Rouge Homme, Lindemans, Tulloch* ■ *The agency needed to provide a contemporary yet classical presentation for these premium, established red wines. The use of elegant dark bottles with clean typography lend a classical elegance. The minimal foil-printed graphics provide a contemporary "sparkle" to the packages.* ● *Für diese anspruchsvollen, etablierten Rotweine wurde eine zeitgemässe und dabei klassische Präsentation gewünscht. Die schlanken, dunklen Flaschen und die klare Typographie sorgen für klassische Eleganz, während die minimalen Graphiken in Foliendruck für einen zeitgemässen 'Funken' der Verpackung sorgen.* ▲ *Le client désirait une présentation à la fois classique et contemporaine pour ces grands vins rouges. L'élégance des bouteilles en verre foncé et la typographie soignée confèrent une touche raffinée et classique à ces crus, tandis que les impressions argentées, discrètes, apportent une touche plus moderne.*

PAGE 133 ART DIRECTOR/DESIGNER: *Jeffrey Caldewey* AGENCY: *Caldewey Design* PRODUCT PHOTOGRAPHER: *Robert Bruno* CLIENT: *Boisset USA* DESIGN/PRODUCTION YEAR: *1996* TYPEFACE: *Architect*

PAGE 134 ART DIRECTOR/DESIGNER: *John Blackburn* AGENCY: *Blackburn's Limited* CLIENT: *Taylor, Fladgate & Yeatman* DESIGN/PRODUCTION YEAR: *1988* BRANDS CARRIED: *Taylors First Estate Port* ■ *The agency wanted to create an exclusive image in a traditional market. The idea of the vertical label came from the "paint mark" traditionally brushed onto port bottles.* ● *Hier ging es darum, in einem traditionellen Markt für einen exklusiven Auftritt zu sorgen. Die Tradition, Port-Flaschen mit einem 'Farbtupfer' zu versehen, lieferte die Idee zu dem vertikalen Etikett.* ▲ *L'objectif était de créer une image originale qui se démarquerait des produits classiques. L'idée d'apposer une étiquette verticale s'inspire des bouteilles de porto qui présentent généralement une marque de peinture.*

PAGE 135 ART DIRECTOR/DESIGNER: *John Blackburn* AGENCY: *Blackburn's Limited* CLIENT: *Allied Domecq* DESIGN/PRODUCTION YEAR: *1985* BRANDS CARRIED: *Cockburn's Tawny Ports–10 & 20 Year Old* ■ *The design is based on the traditional Portuguese bottle featuring acid-etched glass. Torn newsprint labels printed with stain marks and individual numbered bottles were utilized. A wandering Cockburn's stamp changes position from bottle to bottle to suggest hand finishing.* ● *Das Design basiert auf der traditionellen portugiesischen Flasche aus geätztem Glas. Die zerrissenen Etiketten mit Flecken, die einzeln numerierten Flaschen und die unterschiedliche Anbringung des Herstellersiegels sollen den Eindruck von Handarbeit und langer Lagerung vermitteln.* ▲ *Le concept s'inspire des bouteilles portugaises classiques fabriquées avec du verre gravé à l'acide. Les étiquettes tachées et déchirées, l'emplacement variable du sceau du fabricant sur les bouteilles numérotées confèrent une touche artisanale au produit.*

PAGE 136 ART DIRECTOR: *John Blackburn* DESIGNER: *Belinda Duggan* AGENCY: *Blackburn's Limited* ILLUSTRATOR: *John Geary* CLIENT: *Allied Domecq* DESIGN YEAR: *1994* PRODUCTION YEAR: *1995* BRANDS CARRIED: *Harveys Gran Solera Sherry* ■ *The objective was to communicate the prestige of this high-quality sherry sold in duty free shops. The Carthusian horse–spirited and purebred–symbolizes the rarity and breeding of the wine. The unique bottle shape enhances the brand's elegance and distinction.* ● *Die Aufgabe bestand darin, die hervorragende Qualität dieses Sherrys, der in Duty Free Shops angeboten wird, zu unterstreichen. Das temperamentvolle Vollblut symbolisiert die Seltenheit und Rasse des Weines. Die spezielle Form der Flasche unterstreicht Eleganz und Rang der Marke.* ▲ *L'objectif était de souligner la qualité exceptionnelle de ce sherry vendu dans des magasins hors-taxe. L'illustration du pur-sang symbolise la rareté et le goût racé de ce vin. La forme unique de la bouteille renforce l'image haut de gamme de ce cru.*

PAGE 137 AGENCY: *Cato Design Inc.* PRODUCT PHOTOGRAPHER: *Mark Rayner* CLIENT: *T'Gallant* DESIGN/PRODUCTION YEAR: *1994* ■ *The vintage JV VI was a joint venture between six partners, hence the name.* ● *Dieser Jahrgang war das Gemeinschaftserzeugnis von sechs Partnern – daher auch der Name des Weines.* ▲ *Ce millésime est le fruit d'une collaboration entre six associés, d'où le nom du vin.*

PAGE 138 AGENCY: *Cato Design Inc.* PRODUCT PHOTOGRAPHER: *Mark Rayner* CLIENT: *T'Gallant* DESIGN/PRODUCTION YEAR: *1994* ■ *The name T'Gallant means "top sail" in sea lore. The design is inspired by nautical flags.* ● *Der Name T'Gallant, was so viel wie Topsegel bedeutet, stammt aus Seemannsgeschichten. Thema des Designs sind deshalb nautische Flaggen.* ▲ *Le nom T'Gallant, qui signifie approximativement «pavillon haut», trouve son origine dans les histoires de marins et a servi de thème à l'illustration de l'étiquette.*

PAGES 139, 140 AGENCY: *Cato Design Inc.* PRODUCT PHOTOGRAPHER: *Mark Rayner* CLIENT: *Stefano Lubiana Pty Ltd* DESIGN/PRODUCTION YEAR: *1996*

PAGE 141 (TOP LEFT) AGENCY: *Cato Design Inc.* PRODUCT PHOTOGRAPHER: *Mark Rayner* CLIENT: *Mistwood* DESIGN/PRODUCTION YEAR: *1994*

PAGE 141 (TOP RIGHT) AGENCY: *Cato Design Inc.* PRODUCT PHOTOGRAPHER: *Mark Rayner* CLIENT: *Hidden Creek* ■ *The label reflects the location of the vineyard, which is well hidden and guarded by trees.* ● *Das Etikett weist auf die Lage des Weingutes hin, das Bäume vor neugierigen Blicken schützen.* ▲ *L'étiquette se réfère à la situation du vignoble qu'un rideau d'arbres protège des regards indiscrets.*

PAGE 141 (BOTTOM LEFT) AGENCY: *Cato Design Inc.* PRODUCT PHOTOGRAPHER: *Mark Rayner* CLIENT: *T'Gallant* DESIGN/PRODUCTION YEAR: *1994* ■ *The label was designed to appeal to women. The see-through label utilizes the color of the wine.* ● *Das durchsichtige Etikett profitiert von der Farbe des Weins. Es sollten vor allem Frauen angesprochen werden.* ▲ *L'étiquette transparente, s'adressant principalement aux femmes, est mise en valeur par la robe du vin.*

PAGE 141 (BOTTOM RIGHT) AGENCY: *Cato Design Inc.* PRODUCT PHOTOGRAPHER: *Mark Rayner* CLIENT: *T'Gallant* DESIGN/PRODUCTION YEAR: *1994*

PAGE 142 AGENCY: *Cato Design Inc.* PRODUCT PHOTOGRAPHER: *Mark Rayner* CLIENT: *T'Gallant* DESIGN/PRODUCTION YEAR: *1994* ■ *The wine, Pinot Grigio, is unique in Australia. The label was designed to be a contradiction.* ● *Der Wein, ein Pinot Grigio, ist in Australien einzigartig. Das Etikett sollte quasi ein Gegengewicht zu seiner Tradition sein.* ▲ *Ce vin, un pinot gris, est unique en Australie. L'étiquette devait contraster avec l'idée de tradition.*

PAGE 143 AGENCY: *Cato Design Inc.* PRODUCT PHOTOGRAPHER: *Mark Rayner* CLIENT: *Peerick Vineyard* DESIGN/PRODUCTION YEAR: *1996*

PAGE 144 ART DIRECTOR/DESIGNER: *Alain Wannaz* AGENCY: *W, G & R* CLIENT: *Marc-Etienne Dubois* ■ *Label design for Côtes de Provence wine bottles.* ● *Etikett für Côtes de Provence-Weine.* ▲ *Etiquette pour des bouteilles de Côtes de Provence.*

PAGE 145 ART DIRECTOR: *Kristin Breslin Sommese* DESIGNER: *Mike Ballard* AGENCY: *Art 376, Penn State University* PRODUCT PHOTOGRAPHERS: *Richard Ackley, Dwain Harbst* CLIENT: *Self-promotion* DESIGN/PRODUCTION YEAR: *1996* ■

Self-promotion created to be given on Halloween. The box makes the bottle light up like a jack-o-lantern. ● *Geschenkverpackung zum Halloween-Fest in den USA. Die Box lässt die Flasche wie eine Halloween-Laterne (aus einem ausgehöhltem Kürbis geschnitzte Laterne) aufleuchten.* ▲ *Emballage-cadeau créé à l'occasion de la fête d'halloween aux Etats-Unis. Le concept de la boîte permet à la bouteille de briller comme les bougies des citrouilles évidées.*

PAGE 146 ART DIRECTOR/DESIGNER: *Avital Kellner Gazit* AGENCY: *Daedalos* CLIENT: *Golan Heights Winery*

PAGE 147 ART DIRECTOR/DESIGNER: *Avital Kellner Gazit* DESIGN FIRM: *Daedalos* CLIENT: *Golan Heights Winery* DESIGN YEAR: *1995*

PAGES 148, 149 ART DIRECTOR/DESIGNER: *David Lancashire* AGENCY: *David Lancashire Design* ILLUSTRATOR: *David Lancashire* CLIENT: *Self-promotion* ■ *Self-promotional gift of wine produced by the design studio for friends, clients, and suppliers.* ● *Geschenkverpackung für einen Wein, den das Designstudio als Eigenwerbung verwendete.* ▲ *Emballage-cadeau d'un vin utilisé à des fins autopromotionnelles par une agence de design.*

PAGE 150 ART DIRECTOR/DESIGNER: *Mary Lewis* AGENCY: *Lewis Moberly* CLIENT: *Sogrape Vinhos de Portugal* ■ *Packaging for a Portuguese red wine.* ● *Packungsgestaltung für einen portugiesischen Rotwein.* ▲ *Packaging d'un vin rouge portugais.*

PAGE 151 ART DIRECTOR: *Robert Pellegrini* DESIGNER: *Kurt Jennings* AGENCY: *Pellegrini and Associates* CLIENT: *Pellegrini Vineyards* ■ *Packaging for New York wines.* ● *Verpackung für Weine aus dem Staat New York.* ▲ *Packaging conçu pour des vins de l'Etat de New York.*

PAGE 152 ART DIRECTOR/DESIGNER: *Patti Britton* AGENCY: *Britton Design* PRODUCT PHOTOGRAPHER: *Mitch Rice* CLIENT: *Viansa Winery* PRINTER: *Bolling & Finke* TYPEFACE: *Futura Condensed* DESIGN/PRODUCTION YEAR: *1993* ■ *The agency had to create a design for the client's most premium wine which represents a celebration of California civilizations of the past. In this case, a 200-year old arrowhead created by the Native Americans was used.* ● *Hier ging es darum, eine Verpackung für den besten Wein des Kunden zu schaffen, ein Produkt der verschiedenen Zivilisationen Kaliforniens. Als geeignetes Symbol der Vergangenheit wurde eine 200 Jahre alte Pfeilspitze der amerikanischen Ureinwohner gewählt.* ▲ *L'agence avait pour tâche de créer un packaging pour le meilleur cru du client, qui rende hommage aux anciennes civilisations de la Californie. Pour symboliser le passé, l'agence a choisi la pointe d'une flèche utilisée autrefois par les Amérindiens.*

PAGE 153 ART DIRECTOR/DESIGNER: *Patti Britton* AGENCY: *Britton Design* PRODUCT PHOTOGRAPHER: *Mitch Rice* CLIENT: *Galante Vineyards* PRINTER: *Bolling & Finke* TYPEFACE: *Trump* DESIGN YEAR: *1995* PRODUCTION YEAR: *1996* ■ *The land of the client's vineyards combines three subjects–cattle, roses, and wine. To combine these elements, leather was hand-tooled by a California saddlemaker and included a rose border. Silver foil and embossed "conchos" gave the label a western feel.* ● *Auf dem Land des Winzers gibt es nicht nur Reben, sondern auch Rosenfelder und Rinder. Um diese Elemente zu kom-*

binieren, wurde bei einem kalifornischen Sattelmacher handbearbeitetes Leder mit einer Rosenborte bestellt. Silbriger Foliendruck und eingestanzte Rinder geben dem Etikett den gewünschten Western-Touch. ▲ *Les terres de ce client comprennent un vignoble, une roseraie et un élevage de bétail. Pour combiner ces trois éléments, une selle en cuir présentant une couronne de roses a été commandée auprès d'un sellier californien. Les impressions argentées et les bœufs gaufrés sur l'étiquette confèrent un look western.*

PAGE 154 (TOP LEFT) ART DIRECTOR/DESIGNER: *Jeffrey Caldewey* AGENCY: *Caldewey Design* CLIENT: *Zia Cellars* TYPEFACE: *Engravers Gothic*

PAGE 154 (TOP RIGHT) ART DIRECTOR/DESIGNER: *Mary Lewis* AGENCY: *Lewis Moberly* CLIENT: *Sogrape Vinhos de Portugal* ■ *This wine was introduced in celebration of the 50th anniversary of the Mateus brand. The label pays homage to Fernando van Zeller Guedes, the founder, by featuring a cameo portrait. Restrained typography suggests premium quality.* ● *Dieser Wein wurde zum 50jährigen Jubiläum der Mateus-Marke lanciert. Das Etikett mit der Miniatur ist eine Hommage an den Gründer, Fernando van Zeller Guedes. Die zurückhaltende Typographie soll die hohe Qualität der Marke unterstreichen.* ▲ *Vin lancé sur le marché pour les 50 ans de la marque Mateus. L'étiquette à l'effigie de Fernando van Zeller rend hommage au fondateur de la maison. La typographie, discrète, souligne la qualité de la marque.*

PAGE 154 (BOTTOM LEFT) ART DIRECTORS/DESIGNERS: *Enrico Sempi, Antonella Trevisan* AGENCY: *Tangram Strategic Design* ILLUSTRATOR: *Guido Rosa* CLIENT: *Azienda Agricola Bulichella* TYPEFACE: *Jenson Text, Futura Condensed* DESIGN YEAR: *1990* PRODUCTION YEAR: *1991* ■ *The agency utilized the the wine's Tuscan background. An Etruscan amphora defines the geographic origin to Japanese buyers.* ● *Die toskanische Herkunft des Weins lieferte das Thema: dem japanischen Käufer wird sein Ursprungsland durch die etruskische Amphore verdeutlicht.* ▲ *L'agence a pris comme thème l'origine toscane du vin. Une amphore étrusque informe les consommateurs japonais de l'origine de ce cru.*

PAGE 154 (BOTTOM RIGHT) ART DIRECTOR: *Supon Phornirunlit* DESIGNER: *Andrew Berman* AGENCY: *Supon Design Group* CLIENT: *Grand Palace Food International* PRINTER: *BKK Press* TYPEFACE: *Future*

PAGE 155 CREATIVE DIRECTOR: *Primo Angeli* ART DIRECTOR: *Brody Hartman* DESIGNERS: *Brody Hartman, Sara Sandström* AGENCY: *Primo Angeli Inc.* PRODUCT PHOTOGRAPHERS: *Roberto Carra, Jaime Pandolfo* TYPOGRAPHERS: *Brody Hartman, Sara Sandström, Claude Dietrich* CLIENT: *Robert Mondavi Winery* DESIGN YEAR: *1996* ■ *This packaging for a new port wine, available only at the winery, was designed to leverage the new identity established in the redesign of the brand. The design projects an extended awareness of the brand and reinforces the handcrafted, barrel-aged character of this domestic port.* ● *Die Verpackung für einen neuen Portwein, der nur direkt vom Weingut bezogen werden kann, entstand im Rahmen des überarbeiteten Markenauftritts. Bei der Packungsgestaltung ging es um die Betonung der Marke und der Qualität des in Fässern gereiften einheimischen Produktes.*

▲ *Réalisé dans le cadre d'un lifting de l'identité de marque, ce packaging d'un porto pouvant uniquement être acheté chez le vigneron souligne la qualité de ce cru régional élevé en fût.*

PAGE 156 ART DIRECTOR/DESIGNER: *Mary Lewis* AGENCY: *Lewis Moberly* ILLUSTRATOR: *Brian Grimwood* CLIENT: *Asda* ■ The objective was to position this Spanish wine as one to be enjoyed for its character as well as its strength. The bullfighter symbolizes this, and an individual interpretation for each label underscores individual taste. ● *Charakter und Stärke waren das Thema dieser Verpackung für einen spanischen Wein, der von einer Lebensmittelkette in Grossbritannien angeboten wird. Der Stierkämpfer dient als Symbol für diese Eigenschaften.* ▲ *Le packaging devait souligner le caractère de ce vin espagnol distribué par une chaîne de supermarchés britannique. Le toréador symbolise toutes ses qualités.*

PAGE 157 ART DIRECTOR/DESIGNER: *Mary Lewis* AGENCY: *Lewis Moberly* CLIENT: *Asda* ■ Black-and-white typography was used to build on conventional port values and was screened directly onto the bottle. ● *Packungsgestaltung für einen traditionellen Port, der von einer Lebensmittelkette in Grossbritannien angeboten wird. Die Schrift in Schwarz und Weiss wurde im Siebdruckverfahren direkt auf die Flasche gedruckt.* ▲ *Bouteille d'un porto distribué par une chaîne de supermarchés britannique. Sérigraphie sur verre en noir et blanc.*

PAGE 158 (TOP LEFT) ART DIRECTOR/DESIGNER: *Patti Britton* AGENCY: *Britton Design* PRODUCT PHOTOGRAPHER: *Mitch Rice* ILLUSTRATOR: *Georgia Deaver* CLIENT: *Opus One* PRINTER: *Northwestern Graphics* TYPEFACE: *Michelangelo* DESIGN YEAR: *1995* PRODUCTION YEAR: *1996* ■ The label was created as a simple statement. The gold stamped zig-zag mark represents the motion of a baton swirling through the air. ● *Etikett mit einer klaren Botschaft. Das goldfarbene Zickzack-Element bezeichnet die Bewegung eines durch die Luft wirbelnden Taktstockes.* ▲ *Etiquette illustrant le mouvement en zigzag d'une baguette de chef d'orchestre.*

PAGE 158 (TOP RIGHT) ART DIRECTOR/DESIGNER: *Patti Britton* AGENCY: *Britton Design* PRODUCT PHOTOGRAPHER: *Mitch Rice* CLIENT: *Viansa Winery* PRINTER: *Northwestern Graphics* DESIGN/PRODUCTION YEAR: *1996* ■ This wine is a tribute to August Sebastiani, a pioneer in winemaking. This hearty red Italian wine is packaged in a massive Italian bottle, suggestive of Sebastiani. A silver medallion attached to a copper wire finishes off the package. ● *Dieser Wein ist eine Hommage an August Sebastiani, einen Pionier des Weinanbaus. Die Verpackung unterstreicht die Eigenschaften dieses kräftigen italienischen Rotweins. Ein silberfarbenes Medaillon an einem Kupferdraht gibt der Verpackung den letzten Schliff.* ▲ *Ce vin rend hommage à August Sebastiani, pionnier de la viticulture. Le packaging présente les spécificités de ce vin rouge italien riche et ample. Un médaillon argenté attaché à un fil de cuivre apporte la touche finale au packaging.*

PAGE 158 (BOTTOM LEFT) ART DIRECTOR/DESIGNER: *Jeffrey Caldewey* AGENCY: *Caldewey Design* CLIENT: *Arbios Cellars* MANUFACTURER: *RS Design* TYPEFACE: *Centaur* DESIGN/PRODUCTION YEAR: *1996*

PAGE 158 (BOTTOM RIGHT) ART DIRECTOR/DESIGNER: *Rick Tharp* AGENCY: *Tharp Did It* PRODUCT PHOTOGRAPHER: *Stan Cacitti* ILLUSTRATORS: *Tim Girvin, Susan Pate* CLIENT: *Mirassou Vineyards* PRINTER: *Blake Printery* TYPEFACE: *Goudy Oldstyle* DESIGN YEAR: *1995* PRODUCTION YEAR: *1996* ■ The label was redesigned using the signature logotype created ten years ago. The designer made a dramatic statement by designing the memorable label shape based on the red "accent" of the logotype. ● *Das Etikett wurde unter Einbezug des vor zehn Jahren geschaffenen handgeschriebenen Schriftzugs überarbeitet. Dabei bildete der rote «Akzent» des Logos die Grundlage für die spezielle Form des neuen Etiketts.* ▲ *Etiquette reliftée à partir du logotype original datant de dix ans. L'«accent» rouge du logo a servi de base à la forme de l'étiquette.*

PAGE 159 ART DIRECTOR/DESIGNER: *Patti Britton* AGENCY: *Britton Design* PRODUCT PHOTOGRAPHER: *Mitch Rice* ILLUSTRATOR: *Patti Britton* CLIENT: *Racke USA* PRINTER: *Bolling & Finke* TYPEFACE: *Clarendon* DESIGN/PRODUCTION YEAR: *1996* ■ These wines are a limited edition bottling and a tribute to the client's rich heritage as California's first and oldest winery. Using old metal type, "Buena Vista" is debossed into the die-cut label with old newspaper clippings. A copper medallion adorns the top of the bottle. ● *Bei diesen Flaschen handelt es sich um eine begrenzte Auflage für das erste und älteste Weingut Kaliforniens. Der Namenszug in einer alten Bleisatztype sowie das kupferfarbene Medaillon auf dem Etikett unterstreichen die Tradition.* ▲ *Bouteilles fabriquées en série limitée pour le premier vignoble de Californie, qui est aussi le plus ancien. Le nom composé avec des caractères de plomb anciens et le médaillon en cuivre soulignent la tradition de la marque.*

PAGE 160 (TOP) ART DIRECTOR: *Rick Tharp* AGENCY: *Tharp Did It* PRODUCT PHOTOGRAPHER: *Kelly O'Connor* ILLUSTRATOR: *Rick Tharp* CLIENT: *Jory Winery* PRINTER: *Black Hand* MANUFACTURER: *Stillman Brown* TYPEFACE: *Hill Litho* DESIGN/PRODUCTION YEAR: *1993* ■ "Black hand" was a name used by 19th century Spanish anarchists as well as by 20th century Italian-American extortionists. The wine is a synthesis of Spanish and Italian styles and aged in American oak. ● *«Schwarze Hand» war ein Name, der sowohl von den spanischen Anarchisten im 19. Jahrhundert als auch von den italo-amerikanischen Mafia im 20. Jahrhundert verwendet wurde. Der Wein ist eine Synthese spanischer und italienischer Eigenschaften und reift in amerikanischen Eichenfässern.* ▲ *La désignation «Main noire» était utilisée aussi bien par les anarchistes espagnols au XIXe siècle que par la mafia italo-américaine au XXe siécle. Ce vin américain qui rappelle les vins espagnols et italiens est vieilli dans des fûts de chêne.*

PAGE 160 (BOTTOM) ART DIRECTOR/DESIGNER: *Tom Poth* AGENCY: *Hixo* PRODUCT PHOTOGRAPHER: *Richard Krall* ILLUSTRATOR: *Melinda Maniscalco* CLIENT: *Slaughter Leftwich* DESIGN/PRODUCTION YEAR: *1989*

PAGE 161 ART DIRECTOR: *Heide-Rose Metzger* DESIGNER: *Ulrich Metzger* AGENCY: *Metzger & Metzger Werbeagentur GmbH* PRODUCT PHOTOGRAPHER: *Stefan Ellbruck* CLIENT: *Fritz Croissant "Azienda Agricola Vignano"* PRINTER: *KS-Druck* DESIGN YEAR: *1995*

PRODUCTION YEAR: *1996* ■ *Meant for the German market, these bottles were designed for a winery in Tuscany. The agency created a heraldic sign for the client and developed different lines of products. For budget reasons, they decided on a one-color and two-color print.* ● *Ausstattung der für den deutschen Markt bestimmten Erzeugnisse eines biologisch arbeitenden Weinguts in der Toskana. Die Lösung bestand in der Entwicklung eines Hauswappens sowie in der Schaffung unterschiedlicher Produktlinien. Mit Rücksicht auf das Budget entschied man sich für Ein- bzw. Zweifarbendruck.* ▲ *Destinés au marché allemand, ces designs ont été réalisés pour un vignoble de culture biologique en Toscane. L'agence avait pour tâche de créer les armoiries du viticulteur et des lignes de produits distinctes. Pour des raisons budgétaires, on opta tantôt pour une impression unicolore, tantôt bicolore.*

PAGE 162 ART DIRECTOR: *Primo Angeli* DESIGNERS: *Mark Jones, Ray Honda* AGENCY: *Primo Angeli Inc.* PRODUCT PHOTOGRAPHER: *June Fouché* CLIENT: *E & J Gallo Winery* DESIGN YEAR: *1992* ■ *Upscale design created for a champagne line.* ● *Packungsgestaltung für ein gehobenes Champagner-Sortiment.* ▲ *Packaging haut de gamme pour une famille de champagnes.*

PAGE 163 ART DIRECTOR: *John Hornall* DESIGNERS: *John Hornall, Jani Drewfs, Mary Hermes* AGENCY: *Hornall Anderson Design Works, Inc.* PRODUCT PHOTOGRAPHERS: *Kevin Latona, Sylvia South* CLIENT: *Chateau Ste. Michelle Winery* PRINTER: *George Rice & Sons* DESIGN/PRODUCTION YEAR: *1990* ■ *These gift boxes were needed to promote the winery's lesser-known wines and introduce the company to markets in which it had not previously competed. The agency wanted to project a warmth and timelessness that would immediately attract consumer attention and interest.* ● *Diese Geschenkverpackungen waren als Werbung für die weniger bekannten Weine des Winzers gedacht und sollten ihn auch auf bisher nicht belieferten Märkten einführen. Die Lösung bestand in einem Design, das warm und zeitlos wirken sollte, um die spontane Aufmerksamkeit der Konsumenten zu gewinnen.* ▲ *Emballages-cadeau créés pour promouvoir les vins les moins connus du client et lui permettre de se profiler sur de nouveaux marchés. L'agence opta pour un concept séduisant et intemporel à même d'éveiller spontanément l'intérêt des consommateurs.*

PAGE 164 ART DIRECTORS/DESIGNERS: *Wolfram Heidenrich, Michael Buttgereit* AGENCY: *Buttgereit & Heidenrich* PRODUCT PHOTOGRAPHER: *Wolfram Heidenrich* ■ *Wine bottles created for different clients.* ● *Gestaltung von Weinflaschen für verschiedene Auftraggeber.* ▲ *Bouteilles créées pour différents vins.*

PAGE 165 AGENCY: *Chateau la Nerthe* CLIENT: *In-house* DESIGN/PRODUCTION YEAR: *1990*

PAGE 166 ART DIRECTOR/DESIGNER: *Todd Waterbury* AGENCY: *Duffy Design* ILLUSTRATOR: *Todd Waterbury* CLIENT: *Jim Beam Brands* LETTERERS: *Todd Waterbury, Lynn Schulte*

PAGE 172 ART DIRECTOR: *Glenn Tutssel* DESIGNERS: *Nick Hanson, Fiona Burnett* CLIENT: *United Distillers* BRANDS CARRIED: *Gordons, Johnny Walker, Bells* MANUFACTURER: *Walter Sperger* TYPEFACE: *Universe* DESIGN/PRODUCTION

YEAR: *1996* ■ *The year 1996 marked the 150th anniversary of Dewar's. The client commissioned the design of a decanter for the occasion. The design is based on a traditional Scottish brooch and pin and mixes stylish cosmopolitan modernity with traditional celtic motifs.*

PAGE 173 ART DIRECTOR/DESIGNER: *Taku Satoh* AGENCY: *Taku Satoh Design Office* CLIENT: *Takara Shuzo Co., Ltd* PRODUCTION YEAR: *1992*

PAGE 174 ART DIRECTOR/DESIGNER: *Joe Duffy* AGENCY: *Duffy Design* ILLUSTRATOR: *Joe Duffy* CLIENT: *Jim Beam Brands* ■ *The directive was to create a brand identity and packaging for a "small batch" exclusive bourbon.* ● *Hier ging es um den Markenauftritt und die Verpackung für einen exklusiven Bourbon.* ▲ *Identité visuelle et packaging créés pour un bourbon de qualité supérieure.*

PAGE 175 ART DIRECTOR: *Joe Duffy* DESIGNER: *Alan Leusink* AGENCY: *Duffy Design* ILLUSTRATOR: *Bret Meredith* CLIENT: *Jim Beam Brands* ■ *Design for a micro-bourbon produced in limited quantity. The original recipe was created in 1795.* ● *Packungsgestaltung für einen Bourbon, der in kleinen Mengen hergestellt wird. Das Originalrezept stammt aus dem Jahre 1795.* ▲ *Packaging créé pour un bourbon fabriqué en petite quantité d'après une recette originale de 1795.*

PAGE 176 ART DIRECTOR: *Joe Duffy* DESIGNER: *Todd Waterbury* AGENCY: *Duffy Design* ILLUSTRATOR: *Todd Waterbury* CLIENT: *Jim Beam Brands* DESIGN YEAR: *1990* ■ *Label and bottle design for a provocative spirit that incorporates the drinking experience of super premium vodka.* ● *Etikett- und Flaschengestaltung für einen erstklassigen Wodka.* ▲ *Etiquette et bouteille pour une vodka de qualité supérieure.*

PAGE 177 (TOP LEFT) ART DIRECTOR: *Joe Duffy* DESIGNER: *Neil Powell* AGENCY: *Duffy Design* ILLUSTRATOR: *Neil Powell* CLIENT: *Jim Beam Brands* DESIGN YEAR: *1992* ■ *Packaging for a line of Kentucky "small batch" bourbons.* ● *Verpackung für eine Reihe von Kentucky Bourbons, die in kleinen Mengen produziert werden.* ▲ *Packaging conçu pour des bourbons du Kentucky produits en petite quantité.*

PAGE 177 (TOP RIGHT) ART DIRECTORS/DESIGNERS: *Sharon Werner, Todd Waterbury* AGENCY: *Duffy Design* PRODUCT PHOTOGRAPHER: *Geof Kern* CLIENT: *Jim Beam Brands* DESIGN YEAR: *1990*

PAGE 177 (BOTTOM LEFT) ART DIRECTOR: *Joe Duffy* DESIGNER: *Todd Waterbury* AGENCY: *Duffy Design* ILLUSTRATOR: *Todd Waterbury* CLIENT: *Jim Beam Brands* DESIGN YEAR: *1992* ■ *The goal of this packaging was to communicate the peppermint flavor while updating the brand to appeal to a broader consumer base.* ● *Ziel dieser Verpackung war die Betonung des kühlen Pfefferminzgeschmacks. Der Kunde wollte das Image seines Produktes auffrischen und damit ein breiteres Publikum angesprechen.* ▲ *Packaging évoquant le goût frais de la menthe. Le client souhaitait rafraîchir l'image du produit dans le but de séduire un public plus large.*

PAGE 177 (BOTTOM RIGHT) ART DIRECTOR: *Joe Duffy* DESIGNER: *Neil Powell* AGENCY: *Duffy Design* ILLUSTRATOR: *Neil Powell* CLIENT: *Jim Beam Brands* DESIGN YEAR: *1991* BRANDS CARRIED: *Jim Beam Brands* ■ *This label for a new*

schnapps uses American cowboy/cowgirl imagery. ● Etikett für einen neuen Schnaps. ▲ Etiquette d'une nouvelle eau-de-vie.

PAGE 178 ART DIRECTOR: *Joe Duffy* DESIGNER: *Hayley Johnson* AGENCY: *Duffy Design* ILLUSTRATOR: *Hayley Johnson* CLIENT: *Jim Beam Brands* DESIGN YEAR: *1990* ■ The objective of this design was to create a bottle and packaging which looked authentic, like it came from a private stock, with a "backwoods brew" feeling. ● Flasche und Ausstattung sollten so authentisch wirken, als kämen sie aus einer Schwarzbrennerei. ▲ Bouteille et packaging semblant sortir tout droit d'une distillerie artisanale.

PAGE 179 ART DIRECTOR/DESIGNER: *Sharon Werner* AGENCY: *Duffy Design* ILLUSTRATOR: *Sharon Werner* CLIENT: *Jim Beam Brands* DESIGN YEAR: *1992* ■ This packaging was created for a line of Kentucky "small batch" bourbons. ● Verpackung für eine Reihe von Kentucky Bourbons, die in kleinen Mengen produziert werden. ▲ Packaging conçu pour des bourbons du Kentucky produits en petite quantité.

PAGE 180 ART DIRECTOR: *Charles Anderson* DESIGNERS: *Charles Anderson, Daniel Olson* AGENCY: *Charles S. Anderson Design Co.* PRODUCT PHOTOGRAPHER: *Dave Bausman* CLIENT: *Distillerie de Aravis* ■ The cordial label, based on antique postage stamps, was designed to reflect the heritage of this 200-year-old French distillery. Subtle colors, uncoated paper and discreet, classic typography supported the approach. ● Das freundliche Etikett, das auf der Basis von alten Briefmarken entwickelt wurde, sollte die Tradition dieser 200 Jahre alten französischen Brennerei widerspiegeln. Die Lösung bestand in der Verwendung von unaufdringlichen Farben, unbeschichtetem Papier und zurückhaltender, klassischer Typographie. ▲ Inspirée d'anciens timbres-poste, cette étiquette a été créée pour une distillerie française riche d'une tradition bicentenaire. L'agence opta pour des couleurs subtiles, un papier non couché et une typographie classique.

PAGE 181 ART DIRECTOR/DESIGNER: *Ken-Ya Hara* AGENCY: *Nippon Design Center* CLIENT: *The Nikka Whisky Distilling Co., Ltd.* ■ Packaging design for a Japanese whisky. ● Verpackung für einen japanischen Whisky. ▲ Packaging d'un whisky japonais.

PAGE 182 ART DIRECTORS: *Steve Mitchell, Bill Thorburn* DESIGNER: *Chad Hagen* AGENCY: *Thorburn Design* CLIENT: *Millenium* TYPEFACE: *Trade Gothic* COPY: *Matt Elhardt*

PAGE 183 ART DIRECTOR: *Barrie Tucker* DESIGNERS: *Hans Kohla, Nick Mount (Glass)* AGENCY: *Tucker Design* PRODUCT PHOTOGRAPHER: *Simon Vaughan* CLIENT: *Spicers* PRINTER: *Stalley Box Co (gift box); Five Star Press (box sticker)* MANUFACTURER: *Jam Factory Adelaide* TYPEFACE: *Gill Sans* ■ This item was created for a paper merchant as a corporate Christmas gift. Handblown glass bottles were filled with wood-aged fortified Chardonnay. ● Handgeblasene Flaschen für einen in Holzfässern gereiften Chardonnay. Die Geschenkverpackung wurde von einem Papierhändler in Auftrag gegeben. ▲ Bouteilles en verre soufflé pour un chardonnay vieilli en fût. Cadeau publicitaire d'un fabricant de papier à ses clients.

PAGE 184 ART DIRECTOR/DESIGNER: *Barrie Tucker* AGENCY: *Tucker Design* PRODUCT PHOTOGRAPHER: *Simon Vaughan* ILLUSTRATORS: *Jody Tucker (label); Bob Bennett (finished art)* CLIENT: *Southcorp Wines* PRINTER: *Collotype Labels* DESIGN YEAR: *1995* PRODUCTION YEAR: *1996* BRANDS CARRIED: *Seppelt, Penfolds, Seaview, Rouge Homme, Wynns, Lindemans, Tollana, Coldstream Hills* ■ The agency used 500ml clear glass bottles and a contemporary graphic presentation to attract new consumers to brandy. ● Mit dieser 500ml-Flasche aus klarem, weissen Glas und dem modernen Etikett sollten neue Konsumenten gewonnen werden. ▲ Bouteilles en verre blanc de 500 ml et étiquette au graphisme moderne créées pour séduire de nouveaux clients.

PAGE 185 ART DIRECTOR: *Albert Zimmermann* PRODUCT PHOTOGRAPHER: *Albert Zimmermann* CLIENT: *Self-promotion*

PAGE 186 AGENCY: *Claessens International London* CLIENT: *IDV* US DISTRIBUTOR: *Carillon Importers*

PAGE 187 ART DIRECTOR/DESIGNER: *Graham Duffy* AGENCY: *Graphic Partners* PRODUCT PHOTOGRAPHER: *Ian Atkinson* ILLUSTRATOR: *Jim Rogman* CLIENT: *Glenturret Distillers* PRINTER: *Harland of Hull* MANUFACTURER: *Saver Glass* DESIGN YEAR: *1995* PRODUCTION YEAR: *1996*

PAGE 188 ART DIRECTOR: *John Blackburn* DESIGNER: *Belinda Duggan* AGENCY: *Blackburn's Limited* ILLUSTRATOR: *Jean-Paul Tibbles* CLIENT: *Berry Bros & Rudd Ltd.* DESIGN/PRODUCTION YEAR: *1988* BRANDS CARRIED: *Cutty Sark 12-Year-Old Whiskey* ■ The directive was to revitalize the Cutty Sark name in the whiskey market. The record-breaking clipper was used as a theme, "out by the cape, home by the horn." The 12-sided green bottle is a unique, protected brand equity. Twelve illustrations of international ports of call underscore the theme and exploit the shape of the bottle. ● Hier ging es um die Wiederbelebung des Cutty-Sark-Namens im Whiskey-Markt. Als Thema diente der erfahrene Klipper. Die zwölfeckige, grüne Flasche ist ein einzigartiges, geschütztes Markenzeichen. Mit zwölf Darstellungen internationaler Häfen wird die Form der Flasche genutzt, um das Thema wirkungsvoll zu unterstreichen. ▲ L'objectif était de renforcer la notoriété de la marque Cutty Sark sur le marché des whiskys. Le clipper constitue le thème central. La bouteille verte à douze facettes est une exclusivité de la marque. Douze illustrations de ports internationaux déclinent le thème et jouent avec la forme de la bouteille.

PAGE 189 ART DIRECTOR: *John Blackburn* DESIGNER: *Belinda Duggan* AGENCY: *Blackburn's Limited* CLIENT: *Berry Bros & Rudd Ltd.* DESIGN/PRODUCTION YEAR: *1994* BRANDS CARRIED: *The Glenrothes Malt Whiskey* ■ The brand needed a radical new design concept in the notoriously "copycat" malt whiskey market. The unique bottle shape and handwritten label are reminiscent of the taster's bottle in the sample room of the distillery. ● Diese Marke brauchte ein völlig neues Design-Konzept in dem berüchtigen Malt-Whiskey-Markt, in dem Sorten munter kopiert werden. Die spezielle Flaschenform und das handbeschriftete Etikett erinnern an die Degustationsflaschen einer Brennerei. ▲ La marque avait besoin d'un nouveau concept pour se démarquer sur le marché des whiskys maltés envahi par les imita-

tions. La forme spéciale de la bouteille et l'étiquette manuscrite rappellent les bouteilles de dégustation d'une distillerie.

PAGE 190 ART DIRECTOR: *Keizo Matsui* DESIGNERS: *Keizo Matsui, Yuko Araki* AGENCY: *Hundred Design Inc.* CLIENT: *Suntory Co., Ltd.* ∎ This bottle was designed to make drinkers indulge in narcissism. ● *Diese Flasche lässt die Trinker im Narzissmus schwelgen.* ▲ *Bouteille flattant le narcissisme du consommateur.*

PAGE 191 ART DIRECTOR: *Keizo Matsui* DESIGNERS: *Keizo Matsui, Yuko Araki* AGENCY: *Hundred Design Inc.* CLIENT: *The Winery Coop of Ehime Prefecture* ∎ For this local sake, the designer wanted to make an asymmetric bottle which would induce the user to hold and appreciate it from various angles. ● *Der Gedanke hinter dieser asymmetrischen Flasche für einen Sake ist der Wunsch, den Konsumenten dazu zu bringen, die Flasche in die Hand zu nehmen und sie von allen Seiten zu betrachten.* ▲ *Bouteille de saké. Le designer voulait créer un objet asymétrique que l'on ait envie de toucher et d'examiner sous toutes les coutures.*

PAGE 192 ART DIRECTOR: *Mark Wickens* DESIGNER: *Simon Coker* AGENCY: *Wickens Tutt Southgate* PRODUCT PHOTOGRAPHER: *David Gill* CLIENT: *Seagram UK Ltd.* DESIGN/PRODUCTION YEAR: *1993*

PAGE 193 ART DIRECTOR/DESIGNER: *Roger Akroyd* AGENCY: *Michael Peters Ltd.* CLIENT: *Ballantine's* ∎ This premium single malt was developed for the Far Eastern market and was designed to compete with XO Cognacs. The agency created the name, structure, and graphics around the idea that "whiskey is the water of life." The droplet shape represents the purity of both the whiskey and water within it.

PAGE 194 ART DIRECTOR/DESIGNER: *Gary Kollberg* AGENCY: *Kollberg/Johnson Associates* CLIENT: *Austin Nichols* PRINTER: *Kentucky Breed* DESIGN YEAR: *1994* PRODUCTION YEAR: *1995* BRANDS CARRIED: *Wild Turkey, Buckshot, Kentucky Breed* ∎ The directive was to create an original bottle shape, distinctive enough to represent a rare single bourbon while communicating the product as uniquely American. The classic shell design motif prevalent in early American furniture dresses the shoulder. The recessed label presents the namesake. ● *Die Aufgabe bestand in der Schaffung einer speziellen Flaschenform für einen raren Bourbon, wobei zum Ausdruck kommen sollte, dass es sich um ein einzigartiges amerikanisches Produkt handelt. Die Muschel ist ein Motiv, das man häufig bei antiken amerikanischen Möbeln findet.* ▲ *Le client souhaitait une bouteille unique en son genre pour un bourbon rare. L'origine américaine du produit devait également ressortir clairement. Le coquillage est un motif classique qui figure souvent sur les meubles antiques américains.*

PAGE 195 ART DIRECTOR: *Jürgen Schmidt* DESIGNER: *Sibylle Haase* AGENCY: *Atelier Haase & Knels* PRODUCT PHOTOGRAPHER: *Fritz Haase* CLIENT: *B. Grashoff Nachf.* PRINTER: *H. M. Hauschild* MANUFACTURER: *Ormel Vetro, Italy* DESIGN/PRODUCTION YEAR: *1988* ∎ The agency wanted to create a bottle that didn't look like a traditional spirit bottle. The name of the spirit is a play on words–"Nicht" means "nothing" in German. ● *Es sollte eine Flasche geschaffen werden, die nicht wie eine*

herkömmliche Schnapsflasche aussieht. ▲ *Cette bouteille créée pour une eau-de-vie devait se démarquer des bouteilles classiques.*

PAGES 196, 197 ART DIRECTORS/DESIGNERS: *Ron Van Der Vlugt, Rob Verhaart* AGENCY: *Designers Company* STYLIST: *Angelique Van Dam* CLIENT: *Hooghoudt Distillers BV* MANUFACTURER: *Flippo + Schermerhorn* DESIGN/PRODUCTION YEAR: *1995* BRANDS CARRIED: *Kalmoes, Wilhelmus, Royalty* ∎ This packaging corresponds with the initial plans of a advertising campaign. The bottle attire is based on the imaginary associations with the history of the European royal houses (Louis XIV, Marquis de Sade, the church, dungeon, and executioner). The promotional bottles were produced in small quantities. ● *Diese Verpackung entstand im Rahmen einer Kampagne, deren Thema fiktive Assoziationen berühmter Gestalten und Institutionen der europäischen Geschichte sind (Ludwig XIV, Marquis de Sade, die Kirche, Kerker und Henker). Es handelt sich um Flaschen, die in kleinen Mengen als Eigenwerbung hergestellt wurden.* ▲ *Bouteilles créées dans le cadre d'une campagne déclinée sur le thème d'associations fictives avec des personnages et des institutions célèbres de l'histoire européenne (Louis XIV, le marquis de Sade, l'Eglise, les cachots et les bourreaux). Série limitée.*

PAGE 198 ART DIRECTOR/DESIGNER: *Marko Vicic* AGENCY: *Futura* ILLUSTRATOR: *Kostja Gatnik* CLIENT: *Dana Mirna* ∎ Packaging for an orange liqueur. ● *Packungsgestaltung für einen Orangen-Likör.* ▲ *Packaging d'une liqueur à l'orange.*

PAGE 199 ART DIRECTOR: *Charles S. Anderson* DESIGNERS: *Daniel Olson, Charles S. Anderson* AGENCY: *Charles S. Anderson Design Co.* PRODUCT PHOTOGRAPHER: *Dave Bausman* CLIENT: *Distillerie de Aravis*

PAGE 200 ART DIRECTOR: *John Blackburn* DESIGNER: *Belinda Duggan* AGENCY: *Blackburn's Limited* CLIENT: *Rockware Glass* BRANDS CARRIED: *Diomhaird' Eachd Mystery Malt Whiskey* ∎ This bottle was designed as a promotion for the client's new glass plant in Scotland. It is shaped like an antique decanter. The line of text gives clues (sent with the bottle) to the whereabouts of a mysterious distillery that heralds a hidden treasure. The answer to the riddle is the location of the new glass plant at Inverleven. ● *Diese Flasche wurde als Werbung für die neue Glasfabrik des Kunden in Schottland entworfen. Sie hat die Form einer antiken Karaffe.* ▲ *Produit publicitaire conçu pour une nouvelle fabrique de verre écossaise. La bouteille a la forme d'une ancienne carafe.*

PAGE 201 ART DIRECTOR/DESIGNER: *Gérard Billy* AGENCY: *Daedalus Design* PRODUCT PHOTOGRAPHER: *Jacques Villegier* CLIENT: *Societe Slaur* PRINTER: *Imprimerie du Bois de la Dame* TYPEFACE: *Handdrawn, American* ∎ Complete bottle design (including labels, medallion and stopper) for a 15-year-old whisky, targeting mainly the French market. ● *Vollständige Flaschenausstattung für einen 15 Jahre alten Whisky, der vor allem für den französischen Markt bestimmt ist.* ▲ *Bouteille pour un whisky de 15 ans d'âge destiné en priorité au marché français.*

PAGE 202 ART DIRECTORS: *Heather Armstrong, Jonathan Ford, John Mothersole* AGENCY: *Michael Peters Design*

ILLUSTRATORS: *Tom Carnase, Wendell Minor* CLIENT: *House of Seagram* ■ *Product concept for an imported tequila with natural wild herb flavors.* ● *Produktkonzept für einen importierten Tequila mit Kräutergeschmack.* ▲ *Concept développé pour une tequila aux herbes.*

PAGE 203 ART DIRECTOR/DESIGNER: *Glenn Tutssel* AGENCY: *Michael Peters Ltd.* CLIENT: *D'Amico and Partners* ■ *The frosted bottle with ruts of clear glass is intended to suggest purity. The brand name on the back can be viewed by looking through the bottle.* ● *Die Milchglassflasche mit Streifen klaren Glases sollte das Gefühl von Reinheit vermitteln. Der Markenname auf der Rückseite ist durch die klaren Glasstreifen zu erkennen.* ▲ *L'alternance de verre opalin et transparent crée un effet de pureté. Le nom du produit figurant derrière la bouteille peut être lu en transparence.*

PAGE 204 (TOP) ART DIRECTOR/DESIGNER: *Taku Satoh* AGENCY: *Taku Satoh Design Office* CLIENT: *The Nikka Whisky Distilling Co., Ltd.* DESIGN YEAR: *1983* PRODUCTION YEAR: *1984*

PAGE 204 (MIDDLE) ART DIRECTOR/DESIGNER: *Taku Satoh* AGENCY: *Taku Satoh Design Office* CLIENT: *The Nikka Whisky Distilling Co., Ltd.* PRODUCTION YEAR: *1987*

PAGE 204 (BOTTOM) ART DIRECTOR/DESIGNER: *Taku Satoh* AGENCY: *Taku Satoh Design Office* CLIENT: *The Nikka Whisky Distilling Co., Ltd.* PRODUCTION YEAR: *1985*

PAGE 205 ART DIRECTOR: *Jonnathan Ford* DESIGNERS: *Karen Welman, Derek Samuels* AGENCY: *Pearlfisher* PHOTOGRAPHER/ILLUSTRATOR: *Peter Horridge* CLIENT: *Campbell Distillers* ■ *Bottle structure and packaging for a malt whiskey.* ● *Flaschengestaltung und Verpackung für einen Malt Whiskey.* ▲ *Bouteille et packaging d'un whisky malté.*

PAGE 206 DESIGNER: *Alan Colvin* AGENCY: *Duffy Design* CLIENT: *Jim Beam* ■ *This project was commissioned to celebrate the 200th anniversary of Jim Beam. The decanter was designed for a special bourbon and is contained in a gift box that uses elements from the product's history and the decanter design.* ● *Das Projekt stand im Zusammenhang mit dem 200. Geburtstag von Jim Beam. Die Karaffe enthält einen speziellen Bourbon, verpackt in einer Geschenkbox, für deren Design Elemente der Produktgeschichte und die Form der Karaffe verwendet wurden.* ▲ *Projet réalisé à l'occasion du 200ᵉ anniversaire de la marque Jim Beam. La carafe contient un bourbon spécial; la boîte-cadeau illustre des éléments de l'histoire du produit et reprend la forme de la carafe.*

PAGE 207 ART DIRECTORS: *Niklaus Troxler, Käthi Friedl-Studer* DESIGNER: *Niklaus Troxler* AGENCY: *K-Design* PRODUCT PHOTOGRAPHER: *Simon Bolzern* ILLUSTRATOR: *Niklaus Troxler* CLIENT: *Distillerie Studer*

PAGE 208 ART DIRECTOR/DESIGNER: *Mary Lewis* AGENCY: *Lewis Moberly* CLIENT: *Arnold Dettling* DESIGN/PRODUCTION YEAR: *1990* ■ *Kirsch typically is packaged in clear flint standard bottles. The client wanted to break the mold and design a unique bottle. The design takes its inspiration from the black cherry. The colored glass reflects the deep stain of the fruit. The label is applied only on the neck.* ● *Der Auftraggeber wollte als erste Brennerei nicht die*

übliche weisse Flasche für seinen Kirsch verwenden. Das farbige Glas reflektiert die dunkle Farbe der Frucht, und auch das Etikett am Hals der Flasche wurde von der Kirsche inspiriert. ▲ *Pour son kirsch, le client désirait une bouteille unique qui se démarque des traditionnelles bouteilles en verre blanc. Le design joue sur le thème de la cerise, du verre évoquant le rouge profond du fruit à l'étiquette qui orne le col.*

PAGE 209 ART DIRECTOR/DESIGNER: *Ken-Ya Hara* AGENCY: *Nippon Design Center* CLIENT: *The Nikka Whisky Distilling Co., Ltd.*

PAGE 210 (TOP) ART DIRECTOR/DESIGNER: *Gérard Billy* AGENCY: *Daedalus Design* PRODUCT PHOTOGRAPHER: *Jacques Villegier* ILLUSTRATOR: *Cyrille Bartolini* CLIENT: *Cognac Raymound Ragnaud* PRINTER: *Imprimerie Bru* TYPEFACE: *Handdrawn, Caslon* ■ *Complete packaging concept for a cognac targeting primarily the Asian market.* ● *Vollständiges Verpackungskonzept für einen Cognac, der vor allem auf dem asiatischen Markt angeboten wird.* ▲ *Packaging d'un cognac destiné au marché asiatique.*

PAGE 210 (BOTTOM) ART DIRECTOR: *Georges Lachaise* DESIGNER: *Henri Champy* AGENCY: *George Lachaise Design* PRODUCT PHOTOGRAPHER: *Studio Appi, Klaus Ramshorm* CLIENT: *Elie-Arnaud Denoix* PRINTER: *Georges Lachaise* ■ *Package design for the launch of a new brand of liquor.* ● *Packungsgestaltung für die Einführung eines Schnapses.* ▲ *Packaging créé pour le lancement d'une nouvelle eau-de-vie.*

PAGE 211 ART DIRECTOR: *Felix Harnickell* DESIGNER: *Claudia Wilken* AGENCY: *Baxmann & Harnickell* PRODUCT PHOTOGRAPHER: *Stephan Försterling* ILLUSTRATOR: *Dietrich Ebert* CLIENT: *H.C. Asmussen* PRINTER: *Offset Glücksburg* TYPEFACE: *Copperplate, Bembo, English Script Type* ■ *New packaging design for a liquor.* ● *Eine neue Verpackung für einen Schnaps.* ▲ *Nouveau packaging d'une eau-de-vie.*

PAGE 212 ART DIRECTOR/DESIGNER: *Matt Klim* AGENCY: *Klim Design* PRODUCT PHOTOGRAPHER: *Greg Klim* CLIENT: *Casa Cuervo, S.A. de C.V.* PRINTER: *Cameo Crafts* MANUFACTURER: *Vitro Mexico* TYPEFACE: *Handlettering* DESIGN/PRODUCTION YEAR: *1994* BRANDS CARRIED: *Cuervo Especial, Jose Cuervo Tradicional, 1800 Anejo* ■ *This design was created for a tequila to commemorate the 200th anniversary of Casa Cuervo. Old style glass was used in the production of the bottle, with a label design based on Cuervo historical images. Every bottle was hand numbered, dated, and dipped in wax with the family crest impressed in the wax.* ● *Packungsgestaltung für einen Tequila zum 200. Geburtstag der Casa Cuervo. Für die Flasche wurde Glas im alten Stil verwendet, und das Etikett zeigt historische Bilder. Jede Flasche ist handnumeriert, datiert und mit dem Familienwappen versiegelt.* ▲ *Bouteille de téquila créée pour le 200ᵉ anniversaire de la marque Casa Cuervo. Un verre de style ancien a été choisi pour la bouteille, et les étiquettes illustrent des scènes historiques. Chaque bouteille est numérotée à la main, datée et cachetée à la cire avec le sceau de la famille.*

PAGE 213 (TOP LEFT) ART DIRECTOR/DESIGNER: *Keith Harris* AGENCY: *Keith Harris Package Design* ILLUSTRATOR: *Keith Harris* CLIENT: *I.B. Berentzen* TYPEFACE: *Handdrawn, Cheltenham Book* ■ *This new retro-design was created* to increase brand strength by celebrating and emphasizing brand mythology. ● *Dieses neu kreierte, nostalgische Design sollte die Tradition der Marke hervorheben.* ▲ *Nouveau design rétro mettant en avant la longue tradition de la marque.*

PAGE 213 (TOP RIGHT) Art Director/Designer: *Keith Harris* Agency: *Keith Harris Package Design* Illustrator: *Keith Harris* Client: *Lucas Bols* Typeface: *Plantin Bold Cond., Italic, Handdrawn* Brands carried: *Lucas Bols, Godard* ■ This design for a liqueur in the middle-price range was meant to communicate product enjoyment and the distiller's experience and tradition. ● *Flaschengestaltung für einen Likör der mittleren Preisklasse. Das Thema war der Genuss des Produktes und die Erfahrung und Tradition des Herstellers.* ▲ *Packaging d'une liqueur. La bouteille devait donner envie de consommer le produit et souligner la longue tradition du producteur.*

PAGE 213 (BOTTOM LEFT) Art Director: *John Burgess* Designers: *Fabian Schmid, Andrea English* Agency: *Werkhaus Design* Product Photographer: *Jim Linna* Client: *Katahdin Brands* Typeface: *Multiple* Design year: *1995* ■ The agency wanted to develop a fresh approach to luxury vodka branding by emphasizing the vodka's western (Idaho) origin. ● *Hier ging es um ein neues, frisches Image für einen kostbaren Wodka. Die Lösung lag in der Betonung des westlichen Ursprungs: Idaho in den USA.* ▲ *L'objectif était de rafraîchir l'image d'une vodka de qualité supérieure et de souligner l'origine du produit, l'Ouest des Etats-Unis.*

PAGE 213 (BOTTOM RIGHT) Art Director/Designer: *Matt Klim* Agency: *Klim Design* Product Photographer: *Greg Klim* Client: *Casa Cuervo, S.A. de C.V.* Printer: *F P Label* Manufacturer: *Gaasche* Typeface: *Handlettering* Design year: *1995* Production year: *1996* Brands carried: *Cuervo Especial, Jose Cuervo Traditional* ■ The directive was to redesign the bottle for a fine aged tequila. The bottle was designed with a symbolized agave plant debossed into the face. The upscale imagery is enhanced with the use of a gold seal and a gold medallion set into a wooden cap. ● *Die Aufgabe bestand in der Überarbeitung der vorhandenen Flasche für einen alten Tequila. Das Motiv, eine symbolisierte Agave, erscheint erhoben auf der Vorderseite. Das goldene Siegel und das goldene, in die Holzkappe eingelassene Medaillon unterstreichen die anspruchsvolle Qualität.* ▲ *L'agence avait pour tâche de revisiter le design d'une bouteille de tequila réputée. La nouvelle bouteille s'orne d'une agave stylisée. La qualité supérieure du produit est soulignée par le sceau doré et le médaillon serti dans le bouchon en bois.*

PAGE 214 Art Director/Designer: *Mary Lewis* Agency: *Lewis Moberly* Illustrator: *Bill Sanderson* Client: *United Distillers* ■ Label and carton for a malt whisky. The design meant to emphasize authenticity, heritage, quality and distinction. ● *Etikett und Karton für einen Malt-Whisky. Bei der Gestaltung ging es um Authenzität, Tradition und Qualität.* ▲ *Etiquette et carton réalisés pour un whisky malté. Le concept joue sur l'authenticité, la tradition et la qualité du produit.*

PAGE 215 Art Director/Designer: *John Blackburn* Agency: *Blackburn's Limited* Client: *United Distillers* Design/production year: *1989* Brands carried: *Old Parr Elizabethan* ■ The agency needed to create a design for a brand leader. The whiskey was presented in a hand-blown decanter with delicate spiral twists, redolent of the Elizabethan period. The bottle was sealed, then embellished with a pewter cap and frames depicting portraits of three of nine monarchs whose long life "Grand Old Parr" spanned. ● *Packungsgestaltung für einen Marktführer. Der Whiskey wurde in einer handgeblasenen Karaffe im elisabethanischen Stil präsentiert. Die Flasche wurde versiegelt und dann mit einer Zinnkappe und Porträts von Monarchen verziert, die ihr Leben lang Grand Old Parr genossen haben.* ▲ *Packaging réalisé pour une marque leader. Le whisky est présenté dans une carafe en verre soufflé de style élisabéthain. La bouteille cachetée s'orne du portrait de trois monarques, grands amateurs de ce whisky. Le bouchon est en étain.*

PAGE 216 Art Director/Designer: *Matt Klim* Agency: *Klim Design* Product Photographer: *Greg Klim* Client: *Casa Cuervo, S.A. de C.V.* Printer: *Lito Offset Latina* Manufacturer: *Pavisa* Typeface: *Handlettering* Design year: *1995* Production year: *1996* Brands carried: *Cuervo Especial, Jose Cuervo Tradicional* ■ The directive was to design a unique bottle that would contain a first-of-its-kind tequila-based liqueur. The bottle was designed to resemble the agave plant, which is the source of the tequila. The frosted agave leaves surrounding the bottle were meant to contrast with the gloss of the upper bottle. ● *Hier ging es um die Schaffung einer einzigartigen Flasche für einen völlig neuen Schnaps auf Tequila-Basis. Die Lösung bestand in einer Flasche, die an eine Agave erinnert, da Tequila aus Agaven gewonnen wird. Die milchigen Agaveblätter auf der Flasche sollten einen Kontrast zum glänzenden, oberen Teil der Flasche schaffen.* ▲ *Le client souhaitait une bouteille unique en son genre pour sa nouvelle liqueur à base de téquila. La forme de la bouteille rappelle une agave, dont est extraite la téquila. Les feuilles d'agave givrées contrastent avec le haut de la bouteille.*

PAGE 217 Art Directors: *Greg Berman, Peter Sargent* Designers: *Peter Sargent, Greg Berman, Richard Peterson* Agency: *Sargent & Berman* Client: *Osobya Marketing Group* Design year/production year: *1993*

PAGE 218 Designer: *Rob Verhaart* Agency: *Designers Company* Client: *Hooghoudt Distillers B.V.*

PAGE 219 Art Directors: *Jac Coverdale, Heather Cooley* Designer: *Heather Cooley* Agency: *Clarity Coverdale Fury* Photography: *Marc Hauser Photography, Ripsaw Photography* Illustrator: *Stan Watts* Client: *Millennium Import Co.*

PAGE 220 Art Director/Designer: *Mary Lewis* Agency: *Lewis Moberly* Illustrator: *Dan Fern* Client: *Asda* ■ This vodka was positioned as a stylish spirit to appeal to the young, confident, experimental drinker. It was important that it not be seen as a cheaper alternative to the major vodka brands. The silver sickle conveys elegance and coolness. ● *Dieser Wodka sollte vor allem den jungen Konsumenten ansprechen, der bereit ist, ein weniger bekanntes Produkt zu probieren. Dabei durfte der Wodka nicht als billigere Alternative zu den etablierten Marken wirken; die Flasche sollte vielmehr den revolutionären Geist der Jugend zum Ausdruck bringen. Die silberne Sichel vermittelt das Gefühl von Eleganz und Kühle, ganz dem Image des Produktes entsprechend.* ▲

Cette vodka devait cibler en priorité les jeunes consommateurs prêts à essayer un produit moins connu, mais ne devait en aucun cas être associée à une sousmarque. L'image du produit fait appel à l'esprit rebelle de la jeunesse. Le sceau argenté confère élégance et fraîcheur à la bouteille.

PAGE 221 ART DIRECTOR: *John Blackburn* DESIGNERS: *Belinda Cuggan, Glyn Hawkins* AGENCY: *Blackburn's Limited* CLIENT: *Allied Lyons* ■ *Square bottle with corresponding label for a cocktail blend.* ● *Eine viereckige Flasche mit entsprechendem Etikett für eine Cocktailmischung.* ▲ *Bouteille carrée et étiquette coordonnée pour une boisson-cocktail.*

PAGE 222 ART DIRECTOR/DESIGNER: *Graham Duffy* AGENCY: *Graphic Partners* PRODUCT PHOTOGRAPHER: *Ian Atkinson* ILLUSTRATOR: *Jim Gorman* CLIENT: *Allied Domecq* PRINTER: *Holmes MacDougall* MANUFACTURER: *Plm Redfearn* DESIGN YEAR: *1994* PRODUCTION YEAR: *1995* ■ *This comprehensive redesign for a 12-year-old Scotch whiskey utilized elements such as a unique label shape and the "LJ" initials, which were also developed for extension into other point of sale applications.* ● *Diese umfassende Überarbeitung der Präsentation eines 12 Jahre alten Scotch umfasste eine ganz spezielle Etikettform sowie die LJ-Initialen, die sich auch gut für andere Werbemittel in den Läden eignen.* ▲ *Bouteille d'un scotch de 12 ans d'âge. La forme unique de l'étiquette et les initiales LJ, utilisables pour d'autres supports publicitaires, sont le fruit d'un concept entièrement retravaillé.*

PAGE 223 (TOP LEFT) ART DIRECTOR/DESIGNER: *John Blackburn* AGENCY: *Blackburn's Limited* CLIENT: *United Distillers* DESIGN/PRODUCTION YEAR: *1988* BRANDS CARRIED: *Pimms No. 1* ■ *The agency gave this design vitality through rediscovery of the brand's rich heritage, enabling it to compete internationally while reinforcing its "Wimbledon, ascot, and henley" image.* ● *Die Wiederentdeckung der reichen Tradition dieser Marke führte zu einem neuen, frischen Design, das sich im internationalen Markt behaupten konnte.* ▲ *L'agence dynamisa le design du packaging en jouant sur la longue tradition de la marque et permit au produit de s'affirmer sur le marché international.*

PAGE 223 (TOP RIGHT) ART DIRECTOR/DESIGNER: *John Blackburn* AGENCY: *Blackburn's Limited* ILLUSTRATOR: *Matt Thompson* CLIENT: *United Distillers* DESIGN/PRODUCTION YEAR: *1995* BRANDS CARRIED: *Ocumare* ■ *New product development emphasizing Amazonian provenance of a new rum in a market dominated by Caribbean rums. The chameleon, a creature of the Amazon, symbolizes the provenance. It is embossed scampering up the back of the bottle; its head is visible through the debossed "O" on the front. On the label, it appears as a hologram, to change colour and add visual excitement in the club/bar market.* ● *Die Herkunft des Rums aus dem Amazonasgebiet lieferte das Thema für diese Verpackung, zumal der Markt von Rumsorten aus der Karibik dominiert wird. Das Chamäleon, eine Kreatur des Amazonas, symbolisiert die Herkunft. Auf der Vorderseite sieht man eine holographische Version, die ihre Farbe verändert. Die in das Glas geprägte Version des Chamäleons windet sich um die Flasche, wobei der Kopf auf der Rückseite durch den Kreis auf der Vorderseite hindurch sichtbar wird.* ▲ *Packaging d'un*

rhum amazonien qui devait se démarquer sur un marché dominé par les rhums antillais. Le caméléon qui s'enroule autour de la bouteille symbolise l'origine du produit. Sur l'étiquette, le caméléon apparaît également sous forme d'hologramme et change de couleur selon l'inclinaison de la bouteille, un détail propre à séduire les clubs et les bars.

PAGE 223 (BOTTOM LEFT) ART DIRECTOR/DESIGNER: *John Blackburn* AGENCY: *Blackburn's Limited* ILLUSTRATOR: *Alex Hitchin* CLIENT: *Highland Distilleries* DESIGN/PRODUCTION YEAR: *1978* BRANDS CARRIED: *Highland Park Malt Whiskey* ■ *The directive was to create a prestigious image for a high-profile malt companion for the famous Grouse blend. The theme exploits the client's remote Orkney Isles location. The bottle design also incorporates a high-quality finish, an embossed image of barley ears on the neck, and a map of Orkney on the punt.* ● *Die Aufgabe bestand in der Schaffung eines anspruchsvollen Images für eine erstklassige Malt-Qualität des berühmten Grouse-Whiskeys. Das Thema lieferte die Lage der Brennerei: sie befindet sich auf den Orkney Isles und ist damit die nördlichste Brennerei der Welt. Der Hals der Flasche ist ausserdem mit eingeprägten Gerstenkörnern verziert.* ▲ *Création d'une image haut de gamme pour un whisky pur malt de qualité supérieure. Le concept joue sur le lieu de production, l'archipel des Orcades situé au nord de l'Ecosse. Le col de la bouteille est serti de grains d'orge.*

PAGE 223 (BOTTOM RIGHT) ART DIRECTOR/DESIGNER: *John Blackburn* AGENCY: *Blackburn's Limited* CLIENT: *Allied Domecq*

PAGE 224 ART DIRECTORS: *Käthi Friedli-Studer, Ivano Friedli-Studer* DESIGNER: *Käthi Friedli-Studer* AGENCY: *K-Design* PRODUCT PHOTOGRAPHER: *Simon Bolzern* ILLUSTRATOR: *Käthi Friedli-Studer* CLIENT: *Distillerie Studer*

PAGE 225 ART DIRECTOR: *Charles S. Anderson* DESIGNERS: *Charles S. Anderson, Daniel Olson* AGENCY: *Charles S. Anderson Design Co.* PRODUCT PHOTOGRAPHER: *Dave Bausman* CLIENT: *Distillerie de Aravis* ■ *Label design for a unique liqueur.* ● *Etikett für einen speziellen Likör.* ▲ *Etiquette créée pour une cuvée spéciale.*

PAGE 226 (TOP LEFT) ART DIRECTOR/DESIGNER: *Graham Duffy* AGENCY: *Graphic Partners* PRODUCT PHOTOGRAPHER: *Ian Atkinson* ILLUSTRATOR: *Jim Rogman* CLIENT: *Glenturret Distillers* PRINTER: *Harland of Hull* MANUFACTURER: *Saver Glass* DESIGN YEAR: *1995* PRODUCTION YEAR: *1996*

PAGE 226 (TOP RIGHT) ART DIRECTOR/DESIGNER: *Graham Duffy* AGENCY: *Graphic Partners* PRODUCT PHOTOGRAPHER: *Ian Atkinson* ILLUSTRATOR: *Jim Gorman* CLIENT: *Allied Domecq* PRINTER: *Holmes MacDougal* MANUFACTURER: *Plm Redfearn* DESIGN YEAR: *1994* PRODUCTION YEAR: *1995*

PAGE 226 (BOTTOM LEFT) ART DIRECTOR/DESIGNER: *Glyn West* AGENCY: *Market + Design Ltd.* ILLUSTRATOR: *John Beach* CLIENT: *The Gaymer Group Ltd.* ■ *Packaging for a longestablished product made in Holland from brandy and eggs. The directive was to retain a traditional image of quality while updating graphics which had not been changed for over 40 years. Technology also allowed for printing on the bottle rather than on a label.* ● *Verpackung für einen Eierlikör aus Holland. Die Aufmachung, die seit vierzig Jahren nicht verändert* worden war, sollte modernisiert werden, ohne die traditionelle Qualität ausser Acht zu lassen. Dank der modernen Technologie war es möglich, auf ein Etikett zu verzichten und die Flasche direkt zu bedrucken. ▲ *Packaging d'une liqueur aux œufs hollandaise. Inchangée depuis quarante ans, l'image du produit devait être modernisée sans renier l'idée de tradition. Une technique d'impression sur verre a permis de renoncer à l'étiquette.*

PAGE 226 (BOTTOM RIGHT) ART DIRECTOR/DESIGNER: *Ron Van Der Vlugt* AGENCY: *Designers Company* CLIENT: *Hooghoudt Distillers BV* PRINTER: *Söllner + Homburg* MANUFACTURER: *Vetrerie Betti Torion* TYPEFACE: *Handdrawn* DESIGN YEAR: *1995* PRODUCTION YEAR: *1996* BRANDS CARRIED: *Kalmoes, Wilhelmus, Royalty* ■ Jenever has normally been put in stone jars. The client decided to be the first distillery to abandon the jar and use a glass bottle in order to make the product more popular, since the liquor is still associated with exclusivity and is drunk only on special occasions. A tall, dark green square bottle was chosen and burned with a gold/oil solution. Tradition is carried out by using classic typography, combined with handwritten calligraphy. ● *Jenever wird meistens in Steingutflaschen angeboten. Der Kunde wollte stattdessen eine Glasflasche, um das Produkt, das bisher exklusiv wirkte und nur zu speziellen Anlässen gereicht wurde, zugänglicher zu machen. Es wurde eine grosse, eckige, dunkelgrüne Flasche gewählt, wobei die Schrift durch eine Gold-Öl-Lösung eingebrannt wurde. Die Tradition kommt durch die Kombination von klassischer Tpyographie und Handschrift zum Ausdruck.* ▲ *Le Jenever est généralement proposé dans des bouteilles en grès. Le client souhaitait une bouteille en verre pour «casser» l'image trop élitaire de son produit et le rendre accessible à un plus large public. La bouteille vert foncé de forme carrée a été cuite dans une solution or-huile. L'étiquette calligraphiée et la typographie classique soulignent la tradition de la marque.*

Indices

VERZEICHNISSE

INDEX

Creative Directors/Art Directors/Designers

AKROYD, ROGER LONDON, ENGLAND 44 171 229 3424 .... 6, 45, 193

ANDELIN, JERRY SAN FRANCISCO, CA 415 974 6100 .... 40, 41

ANDERSON, CHARLES S. MINNEAPOLIS, MN 612 339 5181 .... 180, 199, 225

ANDERSON, JACK SEATTLE, WA 206 467 5800 78

ANDERSON, LARRY SEATTLE, WA 206 467 5800 78

ANGELI, PRIMO SAN FRANCISCO, CA 415 974 6100 .... 40, 41, 56, 155, 162

ANTISTA, TOM ATLANTA, GA 404 816 3201 .... 35, 37-39, 73, 89, 122

ARAKI, YUKO OSAKA, JAPAN 81 694 67698 .... 118, 119, 190, 191

ARMSTRONG, HEATHER 202

BALLARD, MIKE STATE COLLEGE, PA 814 238 7484 145

BARBOOK, ELAINE LONDON, ENGLAND 44 181 879 7090 24

BASSIE, ANITA PHILADELPHIA, PA 215 546 1995 59

BAUER, JOERG STUTTGART, GERMANY 49 711 210 990 87

BEARD, DAVID LONDON, ENGLAND 44 171 580 9252 44

BERK, EDI LJUBLJANA, SLOVENIA 61 210051 4

BERMAN, ANDREW WASHINGTON DC 202 822 6540 154

BERMAN, GREG SANTA MONICA, CA 310 576 1070 217

BILLY, GÉRARD CEDEX, FRANCE 33 45 95 370 201

BLACKBURN, JOHN LONDON, ENGLAND 44 171 734 7646 ...... 98, 134-136, 188, 189, 200, 201, 215, 221, 223

BLURTON, TONY 74

BOLING, GREGG NASHVILLE, TN 615 244 1818 83

BRANSON-MEYER, BRUCE SEATTLE, WA 206 467 5800 78

BRESLIN SOMMESE, KRISTIN STATE COLLEGE, PA 814 238 7484 .... 120, 123, 125, 145

BRITTON, PATTI SONOMA, CA 707 938 8378 .... 100-103, 152, 153, 158, 159

BROOKS, SHARRIE SAN FRANCISCO, CA 415 621 0915 .... 20, 21

BURGESS, JOHN SEATTLE, WA 206 447 7040 213

BURNETT, FIONA LONDON, ENGLAND 44 171 753 8466 172

BUTTGEREIT, MICHAEL HALTUN, GERMANY 49 2364 9380 0 164

CAHAN, BILL SAN FRANCISCO, CA 415 621 0915 .... 20-23, 90, 91

CALDEWEY, JEFFREY NAPA, CA 707 252 6666 .... 70, 112, 116, 133, 154, 158

CATO, KEN RICHMOND, AUSTRALIA 61 3 9429 6577 .... 52, 53, 55-57, 121, 137-143

CAWRSE, ANDREW SAN FRANCISCO, CA 42

CHAMPY, HENRI BRIVE, FRANCE 33 55 928484 210

CHAN, SHA-MAYNE NEW YORK, NY 212 683 7000 60

CHAPMAN, SHIRLEY FREMONT, CA 510 505 9702 36

CHIARAVALLE, BILL SEATTLE, WA 206 223 0700 25

CHILDS, DON CHICAGO, IL 312 337 0663 43

CHITTENDEN, MARK LONDON, ENGLAND 44 181 879 7090 24

CHOI, STEFANIE SEATTLE, WA 206 223 0700 25

COKER, SIMON LONDON, ENGLAND 44 171 2621707 .... 53, 80, 192

COLVIN, ALAN MINNEAPOLIS, MN 612 321 2333 206

COOLEY, HEATHER MINNEAPOLIS, MN 612 339 3902 219

COVERDALE, JAC MINNEAPOLIS, MN 612 339 3902 219

CUGGAN, BELINDA 221

CURTIS, DAVID SAN FRANCISCO, CA 415 567 4402 .... 43, 86

DASHWOOD, PAOLA 114

DAVIES, PAUL LONDON, ENGLAND 44 171 636 9966 58

DAVIES, STEVE LONDON, ENGLAND 44 171 387 7112 62

DEMARCO, SANDY STATE COLLEGE, PA 814 238 7484 125

DEVLIN-DRISKEL, PATTY SANTA BARBARA, CA 805 963 0734 89

DI DONATO, PETER CHICAGO, IL 43

DOUGLAS, DEBBIE 48

DREWFS, JANI SEATTLE, WA 206 467 5800 163

DUFFY, GRAHAM EDINBURGH, SCOTLAND 44 131 557 3558 .... 187, 222, 226

DUFFY, JOE MINNEAPOLIS, MN 612 321 2333 .... 30, 32, 33, 174-178

DUGGAN, BELINDA LONDON, ENGLAND 44 171 734 7646 .... 136, 188, 189, 200

ENGLISH, ANDREA SEATTLE, WA 206 447 7040 213

FAIRCLOUGH, THOMAS ATLANTA, GA 404 816 3201 .... 35, 37-40, 73, 89

FINKEL, CHARLES SEATTLE, WA 206 440 9036 85

FORD, JONNATHON LONDON, ENGLAND 44 171 603 8666 .... 202, 205

FRIEDLI-STUDER, IVANO ESCHOLZMATT, SWITZERLAND 41 486 1689 224

FRIEDLI-STUDER, KÄTHI ESCHOLZMATT, SWITZERLAND 41 486 1689 .... 207, 224

FUNCK, KAI COLOGNE, GERMANY 49 221 940 3676 75

GERNSHEIMER, JACK BERNVILLE, PA 610 488 7611 26

GIANNATTILIO, LUCI 88

HAASE, SIBYLLE BREMEN, GERMANY 49 42 1323101 195

HADDEN, CHRISTOPHER PORTLAND, ME 207 772 9801 84

HAGEN, CHAD MINNEAPOLIS, MN 612 339 0350 182

HALE, BRUCE SEATTLE, WA 206 440 9036 85

HAMM, GARRICK LONDON, ENGLAND 44 171 753 8466 .... 51, 63, 71

HANSON, NICK LONDON, ENGLAND 44 171 753 8466 172

HARA, KEN-YA TOKYO, JAPAN 81 3 3567 3231 .... 181, 209

HARDENBURGH, DOUG SAN FRANCISCO, CA 415 974 6100 56

HARNICKELL, FELIX HAMBURG, GERMANY 49 40 3553 2812 211

HARRIS, KEITH DÜSSELDORF, GERMANY 211 325587 .... 89, 213

HARTMAN, BRODY SAN FRANCISCO, CA 415 974 6100 .... 54, 155

HASLIP, PAUL ONTARIO, CANADA 416 368 6570 107

HAWKINS, GLYN 221

HEIDENRICH, WOLFRAM HALTUN, GERMANY 49 2364 9380 0 164
HERBERT, LINDSAY LONDON, ENGLAND 44 171 407 4441 110
HERMES, MARY SEATTLE, WA 206 467 5800 163
HERMSEN, JACK DALLAS, TX 972 233 5090 ....69, 81
HOHMANN, BRUNO TROY, MI 810 689 6620 50
HONDA, RAY SAN FRANCISCO, CA 415 974 6100 162
HORNALL, JOHN SEATTLE, WA 206 467 5800 163
HUGHES, DAVID PITTSBURGH, PA 412 281 8077 ....66, 67

IL CHOI, SEUNG NEW YORK, NY 212 683 7000 ....60, 61

JANSEN, RICK SAN FRANCISCO, CA 415 567 4402 43
JENNINGS, KURT 151
JOHNSON, ED FREMONT, CA 510 505 9702 36
JOHNSON, HAYLEY MINNEAPOLIS, MN 612 321 2333 178
JONES, LEON FREMONT, CA 510 505 9702 36
JONES, MARK SAN FRANCISCO, CA 415 974 6100 ....40, 41, 162

KAJIHARA, EMI OSAKA, JAPAN 81 6 941 9618 119
KAMITANI, TOSHIO ASHIYA CITY, JAPAN 81 797 344310 119
KELLNER GAZIT, AVITAL TEL AVIV, ISRAEL 972 3 5245498 ....146, 147
KIYONO, KAHEI TOKYO, JAPAN 81 3 3567 3231 ....76, 77
KLIM, MATT AVON, CT 617 678 1222 ....212, 213, 216
KLOTIA, JOHN NEW YORK, NY 212 683 7000 60
KOBE MINNEAPOLIS, MN 612 321 2333 ....30, 33
KOHLA, HANS ADELAIDE, AUSTRALIA 61 88373061 ....129, 183
KOLLBERG, GARY NEW YORK, NY 212 366 4320 194
KOSAKA, WAYNE SAN FRANCISCO, CA 415 398 9348 117
KUBO, TORU TOKYO, JAPAN 81 3 3567 3231 ....76, 77

LACHAISE, GEORGES BRIVE, FRANCE 33 55 928484 210
LANCASHIRE, DAVID RICHMOND, AUSTRALIA 61 3 942 71766 ....92, 104, 105, 148, 149
LAWRENCE, AMANDA 108
LEHMANN, CHRISTOPHER SAN FRANCISCO, CA 415 255 0125 43
LEMBER, ANDRUS TALLIN, ESTONIA 37 2 631 4335 49
LEUSINK, ALAN MINNEAPOLIS, MN 612 321 2333 ....31-33, 175
LEWIS, MARY LONDON, ENGLAND 44 171 580 9252 ....27, 44, 69, 108, 150, 154, 156, 157, 208, 214, 220
LOGOZ, MICHEL SAINT-SULPICE, SWITZERLAND 44 21 691 8111 115
LOMAS, BRYON STATE COLLEGE, PA 814 238 7484 123

MACLAIN, DAN BERKELEY, CA 510 43 2917 116
MANWARING, MICHAEL SAN FRANCISCO, CA 415 458 8100 113
MARK, JOHN VIENNA, AUSTRIA 431 712 712 4444 64
MAROTA, JOHN ATLANTA, GA 404 816 3201 ....35, 37-40, 73, 89
MARRAPODI, JOE ADELAIDE, AUSTRALIA 61 88373061 126
MATSUI, KEIZO OSAKA, JAPAN 81 69467698 ....118, 119, 190, 191
MCILROY, IAN 48
METZGER, HEIDE-ROSE 161
METZGER, ULRICH 161
MITCHELL, STEVE MINNEAPOLIS, MN 612 339 0350 182
MOTHERSOLE, JOHN 202
MOUNT, NICK EASTWOOD, AUSTRALIA 61 8 373 0616 183
MURPHY, JIM EMERYVILLE, CA 510 653 7400 116

OKUMURA, AKIO OSAKA, JAPAN 81 6 941 9618 119
OLIVER, MARK SANTA BARBARA, CA 805 963 0734 ....89, 111
OLSON, DANIEL MINNEAPOLIS, MN 612 339 5181 ....28, 29, 180, 199, 225
OSBORNE, MICHAEL SAN FRANCISCO, CA 415 255 0125 43

PAGODA, CARLO SAN FRANCISCO, CA 415 974 6100 56
PELLEGRINI, ROBERT NEW YORK, NY 212 925 5151 151
PELLOT, MIGUEL ANGEL SAN JUAN, PUERTO RICO 787 766 7140 65
PEREZ, MIGUEL SAN DIEGO, CA 619 234 6631 34
PETERSON, RICHARD SANTA MONICA, CA 310 576 1070 217
PHORNIRUNLIT, SUPON WASHINGTON DC 202 822 6540 154
PIKAND, RAIN TALLIN, ESTONIA 37 2 631 4335 49
PIRTLE, WOODY NEW YORK, NY 212 683 7000 ....60, 61
POTH, TOM AUSTIN, TX 512 477 0050 160
POWELL, NEIL MINNEAPOLIS, MN 612 321 2333 ....31, 177

RABUFFI, ROSSELLA 109
RAPP, EBERHARD STUTTGART, GERMANY 49 711 210 990 87
REYNOLDS, KIP NEW YORK, NY 212 614 5050 68
ROBERSON, KEVIN SAN FRANCISCO, CA 415 621 0915 ....20-23, 90, 91

SAIMO, DAN SEATTLE, WA 206 447 7040 79
SAKOL, THOMAS PHILADELPHIA, PA 215 546 1995 59
SAMUELS, DEREK LONDON, ENGLAND 44 171 603 8666 205
SANDSTROM, STEVE PORTLAND, OR 503 248 9466 14
SANDSTRÖM, SARA SAN FRANCISCO, CA 415 974 6100 155
SARGENT, PETER SANTA MONICA, CA 310 576 1070 217
SASAKI, YUTAKA TOKYO, JAPAN 81 33567 3231 ....76, 77
SATOH, TAKU TOKYO, JAPAN 81 335467 901 ....82, 173, 204
SCHLOOZ, ELIZABETH 88, 109
SCHMID, FABIAN SEATTLE, WA 206 447 7040 213

Creative Directors/Art Directors/Designers

SCHMIDT, JÜRGEN BREMEN, GERMANY 49 42 1323101 195
SEMPI, ENRICO NOVARA, ITALY 39 321 35662 154
SERRANO, JOSE A. SAN DIEGO, CA 619 234 6631 34
SHARP, GAIL 74
SIBLEY, DON DALLAS, TX 214 969 1050 ....46, 47
SUNDSTAD, JAMES SEATTLE, WA 206 447 7040 79
SUTHERLAND, TOM NEW YORK, NY 212 614 5050 68
SWIETER, JOHN DALLAS, TX 214 720 6020 106

TAYLOR, MELISSA SEATTLE, WA 206 223 0700 25
TEE, JAMES SEATTLE, WA 206 223 0700 25
THARP, RICK LOS GATOS, CA 408 354 6726 ....158, 160
THORBURN, BILL MINNEAPOLIS, MN 612 339 0350 182
TIEKEN, FRED PHOENIX, AZ 602 230 0060 72
TREVISAN, ANTONELLA NOVARA, ITALY 39 321 35662 154
TROXLER, NIKLAUS ESCHOLZMATT, SWITZERLAND 41 486 1689 207
TUCKER, BARRIE ADELAIDE, AUSTRALIA 61 88373061 ....2, 70, 88, 99, 108, 109, 124, 126-132, 183, 184
TUCKER, JODY ADELAIDE, AUSTRALIA 61 88373061 ....2, 99, 124, 127, 128, 130
TUTSSEL, GLENN LONDON, ENGLAND 44 171 753 8466 ....51, 63, 71, 172, 203

UENO, MITSUO OSAKA, JAPAN 81 6 392 8105 119

VAN DER VLUGT, RON AMSTERDAM, THE NETHERLANDS 31 20571 5670 ....196, 197, 226
VENTLING, DEREK AUCKLAND, NEW ZEALAND 54 9 307 0901 114
VENTURA, PIERO 109
VERHAART, ROB AMSTERDAM, THE NETHERLANDS 31 20571 5670 ....196, 197, 218
VICIC, MARKO 198
VOGEL, JIM DALLAS, TX 214 720 6020 106
VOGT, GEORGE 14

WALKER, GRAHAM 48
WANNAZ, ALAIN LAUSANNE, SWITZERLAND 41 21 311 8711 144
WATERBURY, TODD MINNEAPOLIS, MN 612 321 2333 ....166, 176, 177
WELMAN, KAREN LONDON, ENGLAND 44 171 603 8666 205
WELSCH, JEFF SEATTLE, WA 206 223 0700 25
WERNER, SHARON MINNEAPOLIS, MN 612 321 2333 ....177, 179
WEST, GLYN LONDON, ENGLAND 44 171 407 4441 ....110, 226
WESTOVER, RICH STATE COLLEGE, PA 814 238 7484 120
WICKENS, MARK LONDON, ENGLAND 44 171 2621707 ....53, 80, 192
WILKEN, CLAUDIA HAMBURG, GERMANY 49 40 3553280 211
WILSON, MISSY MINNEAPOLIS, MN 612 321 2333 30
WOMBWELL, DAVID LONDON, ENGLAND 44 171 636 9966 58

ZANOLI, JACQUES LAUSANNE, SWITZERLAND 41 21 310 2012 115
ZIMMERMANN, ALBERT ZÜRICH, SWITZERLAND 41 1 42237 185

Design Firms/Advertising Agencies

ANTISTA FAIRCLOUGH DESIGN ATLANTA, GA 404 816 3201 ....35, 37-40, 73, 89, 122
ART 376, PENN STATE UNIVERSITY STATE COLLEGE, PA 814 238 7484 ....120, 123, 125, 145
ATELIER HAASE & KNELS BREMEN, GERMANY 49 42 1323101 ATELIER@HAASE/KNELS.EUNET.DE 195

BAXMANN & HARNICKELL HAMBURG, GERMANY 49 40 3553 280 211
BLACKBURN'S LIMITED LONDON, ENGLAND 44 171 734 7646 ....98, 134-136, 188, 189, 200, 215, 221, 223
BRITTON DESIGN SONOMA, CA 707 938 8378 ....100-103, 152, 153, 158, 159
BRUCE HALE DESIGN SEATTLE, WA 206 440 9036 85
BUTTGEREIT & HEIDENRICH HALTUN, GERMANY 49 2364 9380 0 BUTTGEREIT.HEIDENRICH@KNIPP.DE 164

CAHAN & ASSOCIATES SAN FRANCISCO, CA 415 621 0915 BCAHAN@AOL.COM 20-23, 90, 91
CALDEWEY DESIGN NAPA, CA 707 252 6666 ....70, 112, 116, 133, 154, 158
CATO DESIGN INC. RICHMOND, AUSTRALIA 61 3 9429 6577 CATODES@OZEMAIL.COM.AU 52, 53, 55-57, 121, 137-143
CAWRSE & EFFECT SAN FRANCISCO, CA 42
CHAPMAN & JONES FREMONT, CA 510 505 9702 36
CHARLES S. ANDERSON DESIGN CO. MINNEAPOLIS, MN 612 339 5181 ....180, 199, 225
CHATEAU LA NERTHE CHEATENAUNEUF, FRANCE 33 490837011 165
CHRISTOPHER HADDEN DESIGN PORTLAND, ME 207 772 9801 84
CLAESSENS INTERNATIONAL LONDON LONDON, ENGLAND 186
CLARITY COVERDALE FURY MINNEAPOLIS, MN 612 339 3902 219
COOMES DUDEK TROY, MI 810 689 6620 50
CREATION COMMUNICATION SAINT-SULPICE, SWITZERLAND 41 21 691 8111 115
CREATIVSTUDIO MARK & NEUOSAD VIENNA, AUSTRIA 712 4444 64
CURTIS DESIGN SAN FRANCISCO, CA 415 567 4402 ....43, 86

DAEDALOS TEL AVIV, ISRAEL 972 3 5245498 ....146, 147
DAEDALUS DESIGN 201, 210
DASHWOOD DESIGN AUCKLAND, NEW ZEALAND 54 9 307 0901 114
DAVID LANCASHIRE DESIGN RICHMOND, AUSTRALIA 61 3 942 71766 ....92, 104, 105, 148, 149

Design Firms/Advertising Agencies

DAVIES HALL LONDON, ENGLAND 44 171 387 7112 62

DESIGN IN ACTION LONDON, ENGLAND 44 181 879 7090 24

DESIGNERS COMPANY AMSTERDAM, THE NETHERLANDS 31 20571 5670 DESIGNCO@EURONET.NL........196, 197, 218, 226

DIDONATO ASSOCIATES CHICAGO, IL 43

DIVISION TALLIN, ESTONIA 37 2 631 4335 49

DUFFY DESIGN MINNEAPOLIS, MN 612 321 2333 ....28-33, 166, 174-179, 206

DYE, VAN MOL AND LAWRENCE NASHVILLE, TN 615 244 1818 83

EH6 DESIGN CONSULTANTS EDINBURGH, SCOTLAND 44 131 558 3383 48

EJE SOCIEDAD PUBLICITARIA SAN JUAN, PUERTO RICO 787 766 7140 65

FUNCK KOMMUNIKATIONSDESIGN COLOGNE, GERMANY 49 221 940 3676 75

FUTURA LJUBLJANA, SLOVENIA 386 61 320 350 198

GEORGE LACHAISE DESIGN BRIVE, FRANCE 33 55 928484 210

GRAPHIC PARTNERS EDINBURGH, SCOTLAND 44 131 557 3558 GRAPHIC@DESIGNL.U_NE.CO 187, 222, 226

GROUP M PHILADELPHIA, PA 215 546 1995 59

HERMSEN DESIGN ASSOCIATES DALLAS, TX 972 233 5090 ....69, 81

HIXO AUSTIN, TX 512 477 0050 HIXONINC@AOL.COM 160

HM+E INCORPORATED ONTARIO, CANADA 416 368 6570 107

HORNALL ANDERSON DESIGN WORKS, INC. SEATTLE, WA 206 467 5800 CARBINI@HADW.COM 78, 163

HUNDRED DESIGN INC. OSAKA, JAPAN 81 69467698 ....190, 191

IMMAGINE DESIGN 109

K-DESIGN ESCHOLZMATT, SWITZERLAND 41 486 1689 ....207, 224

KEITH HARRIS PACKAGE DESIGN DÜSSELDORF, GERMANY 49 211 325587 ....89, 213

KEIZO MATSUI & ASSOCIATES OSAKA, JAPAN 81 6 946 7612 ....118, 119

KLIM DESIGN AVON, CT 617 678 1222 ....212, 213, 216

KOLLBERG/JOHNSON ASSOCIATES NEW YORK, NY 212 366 4320 194

KOSAKA DESIGN SAN FRANCISCO, CA 415 398 9348 WKOASIS@AOL.COM 117

KROG LJUBLJANA, SLOVENIA 61 210051 4

LANDOR ASSOCIATES SEATTLE, WA 206 223 0700 25

LANDOR ASSOCIATES, LONDON LONDON, ENGLAND 68

LEONHARDT + KERN STUTTGART, GERMANY 49 711 210 990 87

LEWIS MOBERLY LONDON, ENGLAND 44 171 580 9252 ....27, 44, 69, 108, 150

LEWISMOBERLY@ENTERPRISE.NET 154, 156, 157, 208, 214, 220

MANWARING, MICHAEL SAN FRANCISCO, CA 415 458 8100 113

MARK OLIVER, INC. SANTA BARBARA, CA 805 963 0734 ....89, 111

MARKET + DESIGN LTD. LONDON, ENGLAND 44 171 407 4441 ....110, 226

METZGER & METZGER WERBEAGENTUR GMBH 161

MICHAEL OSBORNE DESIGN SAN FRANCISCO, CA 415 255 0125 43

MICHAEL PETERS DESIGN NEW YORK, NY 202

MICHAEL PETERS LIMITED LONDON, ENGLAND 44 171 229 3424 ....6, 45, 74, 193, 203

MIRES DESIGN SAN DIEGO, CA 619 234 6631 34

NIPPON DESIGN CENTER TOKYO, JAPAN 81 3 3567 3231 ....76, 77, 181, 209

PACKAGING CREATE OSAKA, JAPAN 81 6 942 9618 119

PARTNERS DESIGN, INC. BERNVILLE, PA 610 488 7611 26

PEARLFISHER LONDON, ENGLAND 44 171 603 8666 205

PELLEGRINI AND ASSOCIATES NEW YORK, NY 212 925 5151 151

PENTAGRAM DESIGN NEW YORK, NY 212 683 7000 KOEPFLE@PENTAGRAM.COM 60, 61

POPPE TYSON PITTSBURGH, PA 412 281 8077 DHUGHES@PT.POPPE.COM 66, 67

PRIMO ANGELI INC. SAN FRANCISCO, CA 415 974 6100 JGALEAZZI@PRIMO.COM 40, 41, 56, 155, 162

SARGENT & BERMAN SANTA MONICA, CA 310 576 1070 217

SIBLEY/PETEET DESIGN DALLAS, TX 214 969 1050 SPDALLAS@ONRAMP.NET 46, 47

STERLING GROUP NEW YORK, NY 212 371 1919 54

SUPON DESIGN GROUP WASHINGTON DC 202 822 6540 154

SWIETER DESIGN U.S. DALLAS, TX 214 720 6020 106

TAKU SATOH DESIGN OFFICE TOKYO, JAPAN 81 335467901 ....73, 82, 204

TANGRAM STRATEGIC DESIGN NOVARA, ITALY 39 321 35662 154

TCD CORPORATION ASHIYA CITY, JAPAN 81 797 344310 119

THARP DID IT LOS GATOS, CA 408 354 6726 BYTEME@THARPDIDIT.COM 158, 160

THORBURN DESIGN MINNEAPOLIS, MN 612 339 0350 182

TIEKEN DESIGN AND CREATIVE SERVICES PHOENIX, AZ 602 230 0060 72

TUCKER DESIGN ADELAIDE, AUSTRALIA 61 88373061 ....2, 70, 88, 99, 108, 109, 124, 126-129, 130-132, 183, 184

TUTSSELS LONDON, ENGLAND 44 171 753 8466 TUTSSELS@DIAL.PIPEX.COM 51, 63, 71, 172

W, G & R LAUSANNE, SWITZERLAND 41 21 311 8711 144

WERKHAUS DESIGN SEATTLE, WA 206 447 7040 WERKHAUS.COM 79, 213

WICKENS TUTT SOUTHGATE LONDON, ENGLAND 44 171 262170 MARK_WICKENS@BRANDWTS.COM 53, 80, 192

WIEDEN & KENNEDY 14

ZIGGURAT LONDON, ENGLAND 44 171 636 9966 58

ACKLEY, RICHARD UNIVERSITY PARK, PA 814 865 6507 .... 120, 123, 125, 145
ATKINSON, IAN EDINBURGH, SCOTLAND 44 131 555 2800 .... 187, 222, 226

BACHMANN, RICHARD NEW YORK, NY 212 741 0221 .... 60, 61
BARRETT, FRANCES 74
BARTOLINI, CYRILLE 210
BAUSMAN, DAVE 180, 199, 225
BEACH, JOHN 226
BENNETT, BOB ADELAIDE, AUSTRALIA 618 837 3061 .... 127, 184
BLYTHE, AMY TROY, MI 810 689 6620 50
BOLZERN, SIMON KRIENS, SWITZERLAND 41 340 8270 .... 207, 224
BRITTON, PATTI SONOMA, CA 707 938 8378 .... 103, 159
BRUNO, ROBERT 133
BRUSCH, BEAT LAUSANNE, SWITZERLAND 41 21 310 7160 115
BURNS, JERRY ATLANTA, GA 122

CACITTI, STAN 158
CARNASE, TOM 202
CARRA, ROBERTO 155
CHAPMAN, SHIRLEY FREMONT, CA 501 505 9702 36

DAVIES, STEVE 62
DEAVER, GEORGIA SAN FRANCISCO, CA 415 541 0777 158
DIETRICH, CLAUDE 155
DUFFY, JOE 174
DUKE, LARRY 25

EBERT, DIETRICH REUTLINGEN, GERMANY 49 71 2145747 211
ELLBRÜCK, STEFAN 161

FAWCETT, GODFREY RICHMOND, AUSTRALIA 92
FERN, DAN 220
FORBES, BART 81
FÖRSTERLING, STEPHAN HAMBURG, GERMANY 49 40 390 5839 211
FOUCHÉ, JUNE 40, 41, 162
FREWIN, COLIN 71, 74
FRIEDLI-STUDER, KÄTHI ESCHOLZMATT, SWITZERLAND 41 486 1689 224
FUNCK, KAI 75

GAN, LENA 57
GATNIK, KOSTJA 198
GAUCI, GERARD 107
GEARY , JOHN LONDON, ENGLAND 44 171 603 6132 136
GIGLIOTTI, TOM PITTSBURGH, PA 66, 67
GILL, DAVID LONDON, ENGLAND 44 171 401370 .... 80, 192
GIRVIN, TIM SEATTLE, WA 158
GORMAN, JIM 222, 226
GRIMWOOD, BRIAN 156

HAASE, FRITZ BREMEN, GERMANY 49 42 1323101 195
HARBST, DWAIN UNIVERSITY PARK, PA 814 865 6507 .... 120, 123, 125, 145
HARRIS, KEITH DÜSSELDORF, GERMANY 213
HARTMAN, BRODY 155
HEIDENRICH, WOLFRAM 164
HERBERT, LINDSAY 110
HITCHIN, ALEX KENT, ENGLAND 223
HORRIDGE, PETER SURREY, ENGLAND 80, 205
HOUGH, TOM AUSTIN, TX 512 327 8810 .... 46, 47
HSEHI, JIM 83
HUTCHISON, BRUCE PORTLAND, ME 207 797 3783 84

JAUNDRAU, RAYMOND 69
JOHNSON, HAYLEY 178
JOHNSON, V. COURTLAND 111

KADAK, JAAK TALLIN, ESTONIA 37 2 650 4812 49
KAMITANI, TOSHIO ASHIYA CITY, JAPAN 81 797 344310 119
KEOUGH, STEVE CANBERRA, AUSTRALIA 61 6 2800428 .... 2, 70, 99, 126, 127, 130
KERN, GEOF 177
KLIM, GREG BOSTON, MA 617 737 0434 .... 212, 213, 216
KOBE MINNEAPOLIS, MN 612 320 2333 33
KOENIG, MAGALI LAUSANNE, SWITZERLAND 41 21 310 2012 115
KOHLA, HANS ADELAIDE, AUSTRALIA 618 837 3061 .... 129, 131
KRALL, RICHARD DALLAS, TX 214 823 9878 160

LANCASHIRE, DAVID RICHMOND, AUSTRALIA 104, 105, 148, 149
LATONA, KEVIN SEATTLE, WA 163
LAWRENCE, AMANDA 108
LEHMANN, CHRISTOPHER SAN FRANCISCO, CA 415 255 0125 43
LEUSINK, ALAN MINNEAPOLIS, MN 612 321 2333 32
LINNA, JIM SEATTLE, WA 206 623 2990 .... 79, 213
LO, RICH NAPERVILLE, IL 312 368 8777 43

MACLAIN, DAN BERKELEY, CA 510 843 2917 116
MANISCALCO, MELINDA SAN FRANCISCO, CA 415 905 8236 160

MARC HAUSER PHOTOGRAPHY 219
MARKOW, PAUL PHOENIX, AZ 602 273 7985 72
MARRAPODI, JOE ADELAIDE, AUSTRALIA 618 837 3061 130
MCMACKIN, TOM SEATTLE, WA 206 547 7736 78
MEREDITH, BRET 175
MICHAEL WEST PHOTOGRAPHY ATLANTA, GA 404 892 6263 .... 37, 40
MICHAELS, JEFFREY SAN JOSE, CA 408 434 7014 36
MINOR, WENDELL 202
MITSCHKE, WILLI ULESTERNEUBERG, AUSTRIA 43 2243 785436 64
MOORHOUSE, NEIL 57
MORRIS, ANTON 53, 80

NEWMAN, KEVIN SANTA MONICA, CA 73

O'CONNOR, KELLY LOS GATOS, CA 160
OGDEN, DAVID AUCKLAND, NEW ZEALAND 54 9 303 3707 114
OLSON, PETER PHILADELPHIA, PA 215 972 8790 26

PANDOLFO, JAIME 155
PATE, SUSAN SEATTLE, WA 158
PATRICK, DICK 46, 47
PIKAND, RAIN TALLIN, ESTONIA 37 2 631 4335 49
PIRTLE, WOODY NEW YORK, NY 212 683 7000 .... 60, 61
POWELL, NEIL NEW YORK, NY 212 337 8300 .... 31, 177
PUKSIC, JANET LJUBLJANA, SLOVENIA 4

RAMSHORM, KLAUS BRIVE, FRANCE 33 55 231703 210
RAYNER, MARK HAWTHORN, AUSTRALIA 61 3 9818 3131 .... 52, 53, 55, 56, 121, 137-143
RICE, MITCH SANTA ROSA, CA 707 528 8510 .... 101-103, 152, 153, 158, 159
RIPSAW PHOTOGRAPHY 219
ROBLES, ERNESTO SAN JUAN, PUERTO RICO 787 766 7140 65
ROGMAN, JIM 187, 226
ROSA, GUIDO NOVARA, ITALY 39 32136235 154
ROSE, CLAIRE ADELAIDE, AUSTRALIA 61 88373061 130
RUO, RON 54

SABIN, TRACY SAN DIEGO, CA 619 234 6631 34
SANDERSON, BILL HOUGHTON CAMBS, ENGLAND 44 480 461 506 214
SANDSTRÖM, SARA 155
SCHLOOZ, ELIZABETH ADELAIDE, AUSTRALIA 61 88373061 70
SCHWAB, MICHAEL SAN FRANCISCO, CA 30
SIDWELL, ANTHONY 74
SMITH, MAIRE ADELAIDE, AUSTRALIA 61 88272427 2
SMITH, TAD A. PHOENIX, AZ 602 230 0060 72
SOUTH, SYLVIA SEATTLE, WA 163
STROMBERG, TONY SAN FRANCISCO, CA 415 626 5652 43
STUDIO APPI 210
SULLIVAN, GARY AUCKLAND, NEW ZEALAND 54 9 356 7441 114
SUMMERS, MARK ONTARIO, CANADA 905 689 6219 78
SUNDSTAD, JAMES 79

THARP, RICK LOS GATOS, CA 408 354 6726 160
THOMPSON, MATT LONDON, ENGLAND 44 171 734 7646 223
TIBBLES, JEAN-PAUL SUSSEX, ENGLAND 188
TROXLER, NIKLAUS WILLISAU, SWITZERLAND 41 970 2731 207
TUCKER, BARRIE ADELAIDE, AUSTRALIA 61 88373061 .... 70, 99, 128, 132
TUCKER, EZRA 38, 39
TUCKER, JODY ADELAIDE, AUSTRALIA 61 88373061 .... 99, 108, 124, 127, 184
TUSHAUS, LEO MINNEAPOLIS, MN 612 333 5774 .... 28, 29

VAN DAM, ANGELIQUE AMSTERDAM, THE NETHERLANDS 31 20 6270 630 .... 196, 197
VAUGHAN, SIMON ADELAIDE, AUSTRALIA 61 88212192 .... 124, 128, 129, 131, 132, 183, 184
VILLEGIER, JACQUES FRANCE 33 46 932981 .... 201, 210
VOGEL, JIM 106

WARD, BRION SONOMA, CA 707 938 8487 101
WATERBURY, TODD 166, 176, 177
WATTS, STAN 219
WERNER, SHARON MINNEAPOLIS, MN 612 338 2550 179
WEST, MICHAEL ATLANTA, GA 35, 37-39, 73, 89
WEXEL, DIRK OLAF HAMBURG, GERMANY 179
WICKHAM, M. J. SANTA ROSA, CA 707 526 4632 .... 100, 103
WILTON, NICK 117
WOLFE, BRUCE 40, 41

ZIMMERMANN, ALBERT ZÜRICH, SWITZERLAND 41 142237 185

Clients

ALLIED BREWERIES ... 53
ALLIED DOMECQ BRISTOL, ENGLAND ... 135, 136, 222, 223, 226
ALLIED LYONS ... 221
ANHEUSER-BUSCH, INC. ST. LOUIS, MO ... 35, 37-40, 73, 89
ANTICHE FATTORIE FIORENTINE ITALY ... 109
ARBIOS CELLARS SANTA ROSA, CA ... 158
ARNOLD DETTLING BRUNNEN, SWITZERLAND ... 208
ASAHI BREWERIES, LTD. ... 76, 77
ASDA STORES PLC. LEEDS, ENGLAND ... 58, 108, 156, 157, 220
AUGUST SCHELL BREWERS ... 85
AUSTIN NICHOLS NEW YORK, NY ... 194
AZIENDA AGRICOLA BULICHELLA TORINO, ITALY ... 154

B. GRASHOFF NACHF. BREMEN, GERMANY ... 195
BACARDI MARTINI SAN JUAN, PUERTO RICO ... 65
BALLANTINE'S ... 193
BASS BURTON ON TRENT, ENGLAND ... 27, 44, 63
BERRI RENMARO WINES AUSTRALIA ... 92
BERRY BROS. & RUDD LTD. LONDON, ENGLAND ... 188, 189
BLACK MOUNTAIN BREWING COMPANY ... 72
BLACK SHEEP BREWERY PLC NORTH YORKSHIRE, ENGLAND ... 80
BOISSET USA SAN FRANCISCO, CA ... 20-23, 90, 91, 133
BORDEAUX PRINTERS SAN DIEGO, CA ... 34
BRAUEREI FRANKENHEIM DÜSSELDORF, GERMANY ... 89

CAMPBELL DISTILLERS ... 205
CARLTON & UNITED BREWERIES ... 88
CASA CUERVO, S.A. DE C.V. FRACC. BOSQUE DE LAS LOMAS, MEXICO ... 212, 213, 216
CASCADE BREWERY ... 55
CHATEAU STE. MICHELLE WINERY WOODINVILLE, WA ... 163
COGNAC RAYMOUND RAGNAUD ... 210
COURVOISIER S.A. ... 6

D'AMICO AND PARTNERS ... 203
DANA MIRNA ... 198
DAVID LANCASHIRE DESIGN ... 104, 105
DAVID WYNN WINE COMPANY ... 109
DB BREWERIES LIMITED ... 56
DEL HAIZE ... 68
DISTILLERIE DE ARAVIS LA CLUSAZ, FRANCE ... 180, 199, 225
DISTILLERIE STUDER ESCHOLZMATT, SWITZERLAND ... 207, 224
DOCK STREET BREWING COMPANY ... 59

E & J GALLO WINERY MODESTO, CA ... 162
ELIE-ARNAUD DENOIX ... 210
EMERALD CITY BREWING CO. SEATTLE, WA ... 79

FERRARI-CARANO HEALDSBURG, CA ... 103
FETZER VINEYARDS ... 116
FINE FARE ... 74
FIRESTONE VINEYARD ... 111
FIRESTONE WALKER BREWING CO. LOS OLIVOS, CA ... 89
FLAGSTONE BREWERY ... 28, 29
FLYING FISH BREWING CO. CHERRY HILL, NJ ... 60, 61
FOSTER'S ... 52, 53
FRITZ CROISSANT ... 161

GALANTE VINEYARDS SAUSALITO, CA ... 153
GAMBRINUS COMPANY, THE ... 46, 47
GAYMER GROUP LTD., THE ENGLAND ... 226
GEKKEIKAN ... 119
GLENTURRET DISTILLERS CRIEFF, SCOTLAND UK ... 187, 226
GOLAN HEIGHTS WINERY ISRAEL ... 146, 147
GOOSE ISLAND BEER COMPANY ... 43
GOOSECROSS CELLARS YOUNTVILLE, CA ... 112
GRAND PALACE FOOD INTERNATIONAL THAILAND ... 154
GRENVILLE PRINTING ... 107

H.C. ASMUSSEN ... 211
HAKUTSURU SAKE BREWING CO., LTD. ... 119
HAL RINEY & PARTNERS SAN FRANCISCO, CA ... 40, 41
HANNA WINERY ... 113
HEINZ WEBER LOS ANGELES, CA ... 122
HIDDEN CREEK SOUTHPORT, AUSTRALIA ... 141
HIGHLAND DISTILLERIES GLASGOW, SCOTLAND ... 223
HINKLE VINEYARDS ... 106
HOLSTEN ... 75
HOOGHOUDT DISTILLERS BV GRONINGEN, THE NETHERLANDS ... 196, 197, 218, 226
HOUSE OF SEAGRAM ... 202

I.B. BERENTZEN HASELÜNNE, GERMANY ... 213
IDV ... 186
INCH'S CIDER LTD. ... 51

JACK DANIELS ... 83

Clients

JIM BEAM BRANDS 166, 174-179, 206
JORY WINERY SANTA FE, NM 160

KATAHDIN BRANDS 213
KIRIN BREWERY COMPANY, LIMITED 82
KRATOCHWILL LJUBLJANA, SLOVENIA 4

LUCAS BOLS DÜSSELDORF, GERMANY 213

MARC-ETIENNE DUBOIS 144
MATILDA BAY BREWING COMPANY NORTH FREMANTLE, AUSTRALIA 56
MCKENZIE RIVER CORPORATION/BLACK STAR BEER 14
MILLENIUM 182
MILLENNIUM IMPORT CO. 219
MILLER BREWING COMPANY 43, 54
MIRASSOU VINEYARDS SAN JOSE, CA 158
MISTWOOD VICTORIA, AUSTRALIA 141
MOLSON BREWERY 32
MONTANA WINES 114

NEGOCIANTS NEW ZEALAND AUCKLAND, NEW ZEALAND 2
NEVERSINK BREWERY READING, PA 26
NIKKA WHISKY DISTILLING CO., LTD., THE. 181, 204, 209

OPUS ONE OAKVILLE, CA 158
ORCHID DRINKS 98
ORLANDO WYNDHAM ADELAIDE, AUSTRALIA 99
OSOBYA MARKETING GROUP 217

PADTHAWAY ESTATE 108
PEERICK VINEYARD VICTORIA, AUSTRALIA 143
PELLEGRINI VINEYARDS 151
PENN BREWERY PITTSBURGH, PA 66, 67
PRIVATBRAUEREI FRITZ EGGER UNLERREDLBERG ST. POLTEN, AUSTRIA 64
PROVINS VALAIS 115

RACKE USA SONOMA, CA 159
RHINO CHASERS HUNTINGTON BEACH, CA 78
ROBERT MONDAVI WINERY NAPA, CA 155
ROCKWARE GLASS YORKSHIRE, ENGLAND 200
RUBINOFF IMPORTING CO., INC. 69, 81

SADDLER'S CREEK WINERY POKOLBIN, AUSTRALIA 126, 127
SAINSBURY'S 62
SAKU BREWERY, LTD. 49
SAMUEL SMITH & SON P/L ANGASTON, AUSTRALIA 128, 130
SCHWABEN BRÄU ROB. LEICHT KG 87
SCOTTISH COURAGE 24
SEAGRAM UK LTD. HAMMERSMITH, ENGLAND 192
SHIPYARD BREWING CO. PORTLAND, ME 84
SIBRA S.A. FAIBOURG, SWITZERLAND 45
SLAUGHTER LEFTWICH 160
SOCIETE SLAUR 201
SOGRAPE VINHOS DE PORTUGAL VILA NOVA DE GAIA, PORTUGAL 150, 154
SOUTH AUSTRALIAN BREWING CO., THE ADELAIDE, AUSTRALIA 70
SOUTH PACIFIC BREWERY 57
SOUTHCORP WINES SYDNEY, AUSTRALIA 124, 129, 131, 132, 184
SPICERS 183
ST. STAN'S BREWING CO. 43
STEFANO LUBIANA PTY. LTD. TASMANIA, AUSTRALIA 139, 140
STONEY CREEK ROCHESTER, MI 50
STRAPRAMEN BREWERY DRABUE, CZECH REPUBLIC 70
STROH BREWERY, THE DETROIT, MI 30, 31, 33, 86
SUNTORY CO., LTD. OSAKA, JAPAN 190

TAKARA SHUZO CO., LTD 173
TAYLOR, FLADGATE & YEATMAN VILA NOVA DE GAIA, PORTUGAL 134
TENNENT CALEDONIAN BREWERIES 48, 71
TESCO STORES LTD. 69, 110
T'GALLANT VICTORIA, AUSTRALIA 137, 138, 141, 142

UNITED DISTILLERS LONDON, ENGLAND 172, 214, 215, 223

VIANSA WINERY SONOMA, CA 100-103, 152, 158
VINEFERA SERVICES PTY LTD AUSTRALIA 121

WINERY COOP OF EHIME PREFECTURE, THE EHIME, JAPAN 191

YAGI SHIZOU-BU 118, 119
YARDEN 147
YOSEMITE BREWING COMPANY MARIPOSA, CA 36

ZACA MESA WINERY 117
ZIA CELLARS NAPA, CA 154

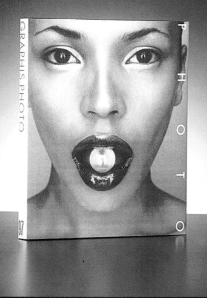

GRAPHIS PHOTO

PHOTO

97

GRAPHIS POSTER

POSTER

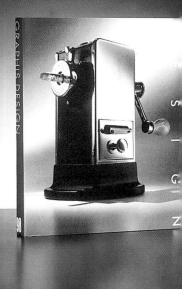

GRAPHIS DESIGN

DESIGN

99

GRAPHIS ADVERTISING

ADVERTISING

98

GRAPHIS BROCHURES

BROCHURES

2

GRAPHIS PACKAGING

PACKAGING

97

SIGNS OF THE TIMES

SIGNS

OF THE

TIMES

GRAPHIS PRODUCT DESIGN

PRODUCT DESIGN

2

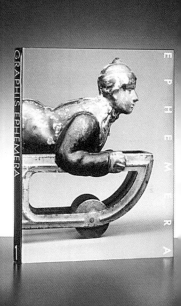

GRAPHIS EPHEMERA

EPHEMERA

1